UNBURDENED BY CONSCIENCE

A Black People's Collective Account of America's Ante-Bellum South and the Aftermath

REVISED EDITION

Anthony W. Neal

University Press of America,® Inc.
Lanham · Boulder · New York · Toronto · Plymouth, UK

Copyright © 2010 by
University Press of America,® Inc.
4501 Forbes Boulevard
Suite 200
Lanham, Maryland 20706
UPA Acquisitions Department (301) 459-3366

Estover Road
Plymouth PL6 7PY
United Kingdom

Library of Congress Control Number: 2009938676
ISBN: 978-0-7618-4965-0 (paperback : alk. paper)
eISBN: 978-0-7618-4966-7

⊖™ The paper used in this publication meets the minimum
requirements of American National Standard for Information
Sciences—Permanence of Paper for Printed Library Materials,
ANSI Z39.48-1992

In Memory of Lloyd E. Hart Jr.

Affectionately Known as "The Book Man"
In Boston's Black Community

Contents

*As long as the lion writes the elephant's history,
the lion will always be king of the jungle.*

African Proverb

Preface

A lmost thirty years ago while pursuing my bachelor of arts degree in college, I took a lot of black studies courses, having developed a thirst for the study of my history. During that time, I also elected courses on the history of American slavery. Like most of the classes that I took in college, I recall sitting in those American slavery classes surrounded by white students. The classes were taught by white professors as well, who assigned history textbooks written mostly by Caucasian historians. They included Ulrich B. Phillips, Kenneth M. Stampp, Stanley M. Elkins, Gerald Mullin, Eugene D. Genovese, Robert W. Fogel, and Stanley L. Engerman.

With the exception of a few, those historians offered an essentially unapologetic Southern view of American slavery; it was a benign institution. They focused primarily on the slaveholders, whom they euphemistically called "Southern planters." Although each historian chose different words to convey his message about the slaveowners, the message was almost always the same: Brutal and inhuman masters were exceptions to the general rule. The majority of Southern planters were good people who were morally concerned about the welfare of their slaves. Enslaved blacks suffered less than any other class in the ante-bellum South because they were well cared for and adequately fed by their owners. Masters pursued a policy of kindness whenever possible, offering their slaves rewards and positive incentives for good behavior.

The few historians who acknowledged the cruel suffering that black people endured under the American slavery regime insisted that whatever wrongdoing the slaveholders had committed was understandable within the context of their society. Others told us that some masters who were forced to physically "correct" their disobedient slaves were defensive and apologetic about it.

As I read those history textbooks about American slavery, it dawned on me that I was not the intended audience. From the information those historians had presented, I quickly gathered that they were offering feel-better-about-the-past history—written primarily for my white classmates. Some of the required reading that my professors had assigned offered us irrational arguments and explanations for the prolonged enslavement of black people: American slavery was the best school yet invented for the mass training of blacks, who were slow and backward. Since Africans in America had no appreciation for freedom and independence, they could gain it only through acculturation—by adopting the culture and values of Europeans.

After completing my assigned reading, I harbored a deep resentment because I believed that I had been required to read propaganda for academic credit. It also was apparent to me that in trying to humanize the slaveholders, most of those historians were leaving out an indispensable part of their record: the slaveowners' countless acts of murder, their disturbing use of torture, and the fear with which that filled their slaves.

Why was the American slavery regime able to survive for so long? Was it really because enslaved blacks were well cared for and adequately fed by their owners and believed them to be good people? Was it because Africans in America had no appreciation for freedom and independence? I felt compelled to offer another viewpoint on American slavery—a black people's perspective. After all, what people are better qualified to provide a true and accurate account of slavery in the United States than those former slaves who endured it? I conducted my own research, reading innumerable slave narratives and contemporaneous accounts of American slavery. My ancestors left behind a considerable record. Some revealed horrendous acts committed by slaveholders— things rarely discussed in the American slavery history books that we had been required to read in college. Indeed, courageous former slaves such as Henry Johnson, Ben Simpson, Rose Williams, and others exposed the full horrors of American slavery at a time when it might have placed them in danger for having done so. Determined to present slavery from their point of view—to provide a black people's collective account of America's ante-bellum South—I offer this book as the product of that effort.

This work is divided into four sections. In Part One, I examine historiography on the brutality of American slavery. I then permit the ex-slaves to speak for themselves, revealing the forms of torture used by the slaveholding class and showing how that torture, the repressive slave codes, and the omnipresent slave patrols instilled fear in the slave community and prevented widespread slave revolts. Because master-on-slave rape and the slaveholders' practice of slave breeding have never been fully explored in most history books about American slavery, those matters are examined in Part Two. In Part Three, I discuss the break-up of slave marital unions and slave families, taking into account what influential historians have written about the subject and also incorporating what ex-slaves have told us about it. In Part Four, I address the aftermath of American slavery, arguing that post-Reconstruction, twentieth-century, and present-day forms of white violence, repression, and racial discrimination have hindered and continue to impede black social and economic progress.

I am forever indebted to Professor Robert Johnson Jr. of the University of

Massachusetts-Boston for reviewing my manuscript and encouraging me to publish it. I thank W. Paul Coates for providing invaluable criticism. I also thank Professor Wilson J. Moses whose stimulating lectures during my college years helped me to develop a love of African-American history. I express my appreciation to Susan L. Glover and Sean Casey of the Department of Rare Books at the Copley Square branch of the Boston Public Library. I also thank Christopher Keck for editing an early draft of my manuscript. I am grateful to Kalimah Rahim for her suggestions. Special thanks are due to Suzan Gervais of the John D. Rockefeller Library at Brown University for her help and to Darlene Thompson and Robin Elaine Ifill as well for reading early drafts of my manuscript. Finally, I thank Eva Kerr for editing the final draft of my work.

Anthony W. Neal
Boston, Massachusetts
August 1, 2008

PART ONE

Brutality and Physical Repression

CHAPTER ONE

Scholarship on the Brutality of American Slavery

"As long as we rely on white historians to write black history for us, we should keep silent about what they produce."

—CHANCELLOR WILLIAMS,
The Destruction of Black Civilization, 1975

S lavery in America's ante-bellum South was a brutal regime that damaged the health of black people. They experienced psychological and emotional trauma, but the worst damage inflicted upon them by their white captors was physical. Unfortunately, American historians as a group have been unwilling to expose the full horrors of American slavery. They have concealed the slaveholders' violent acts. Most pre-civil rights era scholarship denies that any physical cruelty ever existed and is overly tolerant of the Southern view that slavery was a benign institution. Other studies, though maintaining that American slavery was a repressive regime, give too much credence to the view that slaveholders offered positive incentives as a primary means of securing their slaves' obedience.

The want of objective scholarship on the true brutality of American slavery may be traced back to an important but racially-biased study published in the early twentieth century.[1] In *American Negro Slavery* (1918), Ulrich Bonnell Phillips (1877-1934), a white Southerner who was the first major historian of American slavery, denied that considerable brutality existed under the institution.[2] "In the actual regime severity was clearly the exception," he wrote, "and kindliness the rule." According to Phillips, American slavery was by no means a cruel and inhumane system but "on the whole . . . the best schools yet invented for the mass training of that sort of inert and backward people which the bulk of the American negroes represented."[3] At the time of his death, he stood as the foremost authority on American slavery.

Writing during the late 1940s and early 1950s, Samuel Eliot Morison

(1887-1976) and Henry Steele Commager (1902-1998) also were overly tolerant of the Southern view that slavery was a benign institution and Africans in America were content with their lot. In their view, "Sambo" suffered less than any other class in the South, and most slaves "were adequately fed, well cared for, and apparently happy."[4]

Kenneth M. Stampp's *Peculiar Institution* (1956) was one of the first major works to challenge that view. Stampp asserted that slavery was an oppressive institution and the characteristic mode of adjustment was one of resistance. This resistance manifested itself as the slaves made themselves troublesome property. Stampp found that the slaveholder typically attempted to accustom his slave to rigid discipline, "demand from him unconditional submission, impress upon him his innate inferiority, develop in him a paralyzing fear of white men, train him to adopt the master's code of good behavior, and instill in him a sense of total dependence."[5] While Stampp recognized these forms of control, he nonetheless saw religious instruction as the master's primary means of securing unconditional submission[6] and his benevolence as a second way.[7] Depicting the slaveholder in this more favorable light, he placed physical coercion low on the ladder of inducement.[8] Although Stampp conceded that bondage could not have existed without the power to torture, he focused primarily on the master's non-coercive methods of securing obedience—measures which were neither as important as violence nor as effective as it in sustaining and prolonging the evil regime.

Stampp acknowledged that American slavery was characterized by violence, which is an important first step, but he did not take a stand on the degree of brutality, claiming that records were fragmentary and sometimes hinted only vaguely at conditions.[9] As we will see, the innumerable acts of cruelty, documented in both the wealth of slave testimony and travelers' contemporaneous accounts, suggest that Stampp was unwilling to fully research or investigate the brutality suffered by those who he would have us believe were the "voiceless solitudes."[10]

In 1959, Stanley M. Elkins published *Slavery: A Problem in American Institutional and Intellectual Life*. He argued that slavery was so degrading, traumatic, and brutalizing that it forever crippled black people. According to him, Africans were what slavery had made them; a working adjustment to the institution of American slavery required a childlike conformity and a limited choice of significant others. Elkins offered what he called a "German concentration camp" analogy, reasoning that to survive in the plantation system, out of necessity, the slave had to in some way picture his master as the good father. In his view, the mechanism that inspired devotion was not "the cruelty of the parent but rather the abnormal dependency of the child."[11]

Scholars who have completed advanced studies in the field must know that American slavery was characterized by violence. Nonetheless, though they had to be aware of the horrible torment Africans endured at the hands of their white captors, many American historians have defensively engaged in rationalization and denial. Although they have struggled to offer convincing explanations for the slaves' prolonged bondage, some are reluctant to concede that the masters' physical cruelty was its chief cause.

Widespread acceptance of Elkins's notion that black slaves were abnormally dependent children promoted the belief that the blame for their continued bondage fell not on the slaveholding class, but on the Africans themselves. Nevertheless, Elkins is credited for acknowledging the brutality of American slavery. Violence was ever-present. It was part of the slave's daily existence. The whippings, body mutilations, and killings created real terror, and the fear it implanted in black people—not a childlike devotion—kept the slave system intact.

In 1972, Gerald Mullin completed a provocative study entitled *Flight and Rebellion.*[12] He maintained that a gradual transformation of traditional African values, or a cultural change, made blacks less suitable for plantation slavery. The assimilation or acculturation process gave rise to rebellious qualities in the slaves. Simply stated, Mullin suggested that Africans gained a greater appreciation for freedom and independence by adopting the culture and values of Europeans. He also believed that American slavery was a benign institution. In his study, he chose to call the slaveholder a patriarch who served as an accomplished head of an extended plantation family.

Mullin, among other historians, used the word "punishment" to describe the horrific torture Africans endured. In the dictionary, punishment is defined as "undergoing suffering, pain, or loss that serves as retribution, or having a penalty inflicted or imposed on an offender." In the context of the master-slave relationship, use of the word assigns fault to the slave as offender. It suggests that black people who behaved in a manner unacceptable to their white captors deserved physical "correction,"[13] and it renders various forms of torture acceptable.[14] Once torture is recast as punishment, instead of faulting the slaveholder for torturing his slaves, Mullin is able to shift his focus and surmise that one slaveholder's "mischievous servants craved physical correction."[15] The immoral slave codes of the Old South defined resistance to unnatural subjugation as an offense, but enslaved Africans in America committed no wrongdoing when they offered resistance—when they refused to passively accept their captivity.

Because American historians writing in the 1970s also gave little attention to the brutal aspects of American slavery, they underestimated the estrangement, the horror, and the violence that characterized the process of enslavement. John W. Blassingame's *Slave Community,*[16] George P. Rawick's *From Sundown to Sunup,*[17] and Lawrence W. Levine's *Black Culture and Black Consciousness*[18] focused on the slave's creative instinct and the cultural richness of his community.

With few exceptions, American scholars had expressed the view that since slavery in the United States wiped out all linguistic and institutional aspects of African life, it also wiped out all elements of traditional West African culture. The sociologist E. Franklin Frazier, for example, wrote, "In America there was no social organization to sustain whatever ideas and conceptions of life the

Negro slave might have retained of his African heritage."[19] But Rawick subsequently pointed out that "culture and personality are not like old clothes that can be taken off and thrown away,"[20] and Levine maintained that culture can be "expressed as well by something less tangible" such as a "shared fundamental outlook toward the past, present and future and a common means of cultural expression."[21]

Undoubtedly, the slave's ordeal in America did not totally destroy his African culture. The American slavery regime did leave space for some cultural independence and a modicum of self-respect. The late historian John W. Blassingame found that the African in America retained elements of his native tongue, native folk tales, native song and dance, and African religious rites.[22] Indeed, he argued that the slaves were able to develop their own cultural forms of expression, and they did establish viable culturally autonomous communities under the American slavery regime. But by focusing on the cultural richness of the slave community, these respected scholars set themselves up for the economic historians Robert W. Fogel and Stanley L. Engerman who, under the guise of "scientific" research, brazenly downplayed the slaveholder's barbarity, created a favorable picture of American slavery, and arguably, defended the regime.[23] In their opinion, whipping was a fully acceptable form of torture, most masters were not malicious, brutal, or sadistic, and some developed a wide-ranging system of rewards, including "elaborate schemes for profit-sharing with their slaves."[24]

The historian Eugene D. Genovese, probably one of the foremost authorities on American slavery, also devoted less attention to the brutal aspects of slavery by focusing on the living space created for the slave by the so-called paternalistic compromise. This compromise consisted of reciprocal obligations: the slave internalized the role of a dependent child who was expected to accept "punishment" from his master, and his master, the "parent," was expected to administer the punishment non-arbitrarily and in a coolly calculated manner.[25] The historian James Oakes elaborated on the paternalistic ethos. He maintained that the slaveholder believed philosophically that he was at the top of a natural, immutable, and divinely inspired social order wherein he never neglected his responsibilities as the head of his household and ideally "ruled his estate with generosity, providing for the material needs of family and servants, never resorting to harsh treatment."[26]

In Genovese's view, paternalism was a significant factor in keeping the American slavery system intact.[27] He missed the mark. Black people were not disobedient children; they were captives who were lawfully kept ignorant,[28] tortured, and forced to provide labor against their will. Africans in America were powerless to revolt against a regime that gave the slaveholder license to "punish" his slaves by savagely whipping, mutilating, or killing them. Although Genovese insisted that paternalism helped to prolong the survival of the American slavery regime, he did concede that "masters and overseers undoubtedly murdered more slaves than we will ever know," and "arrests, convictions and punishment never remotely kept pace with the number of victims."[29] If the latter is true, enslaved blacks in the ante-bellum South must have found the murder of more slaves than we will ever know a major deterrent to resistance and a horrifying reminder of the consequences of rebellion.

Downplaying the cruelty, Genovese wrote, "Slaves in the United States probably suffered the ultimate crime of violence less frequently than did those in other American slave societies, and white killers probably faced justice more often in the Old South than elsewhere."[30] However, there were historians, notably Rhett S. Jones, who disagreed. Jones found that slavery was crueler in North America than in the Caribbean and South America, and that "this cruelty grew out of the social organization of what was later to become the United States."[31] Stanley Elkins was also aware that in the ante-bellum South the murder of slaves was not punishable in ways applying to white society because the law prohibited black people from testifying in the courts.[32]

In 1989, Peter J. Parish published *Slavery: History and Historians*. He argued that the master had competing needs for profit and paternalism which were not mutually exclusive in his mind. In defense of the master's good character, Parish contended that the slaveholder's relentless pursuit of profit was tempered or "restrained by the conventional morality of his time, his own standards of decency, the precepts of his religious faith, and the pressure of the white community." In Parish's view, torture and positive incentives were combined and balanced in one system of management and discipline.[33] Moreover, he found that the master's self-interest in increasing the population of his most valuable asset—his slaves—forced him to provide at least minimal material and social conditions which would encourage or at least not hinder slave childbearing.[34] To his credit, Parish acknowledged nonetheless that the use or threat of torture was fundamental to the survival of American slavery regime and all other methods—including the use of rewards and incentives—were secondary.[35]

In 2002, John C. Perry, a white Southerner, published *Myths & Realities of American Slavery*. A disciple of Ulrich B. Phillips, he insists that masters applied no policy of brutality and asks why slaveholders would risk the potential physical harm by severely whipping their slaves?[36] The short answer is that masters risked physically injuring their slaves because they understood that administering severe whippings was the most effective method of extracting efficient slave labor. After all, what real incentive did the slaves have to work very hard, and how else were the slaveholders going to reap the benefit of the bargain? Enslaved black people in America felt no compulsion to overwork themselves unless forced to by application of the slave driver's lash. Unless they severely whipped their slaves, the slaveholders would not have commanded a profitable return on their cash investment in human property. The most barbarous cruelty existed on those plantations where masters employed overseers to torture their slaves because overseers were generally ruthless in their treatment of slaves.[37] The ninety-year-old Virginia ex-slave Silas Jackson recalled that "slaves were driven at top speed and whipped at the snap of a finger by the overseers."[38]

The slaveowner was able to risk physically harming his slaves because he also realized that no white Southerner would ever hold him accountable for murdering them. Indeed, many masters in the ante-bellum South placed the health of their slaves second to the success of their harvest. There were slaveholders who whipped their slaves to death for not working as productively as they expected them to work.[39]

Perry also maintains that the more common form of motivation was not the practice of torture, but a system of rewards. Some slaves, Perry argues, participated in "the forerunner of a modern corporate bonus plan": the slaveholders generally shared profits with their slaves. He claims that the most popular rewards slaveowners gave their captives at the end of each year were cash bonuses—some quite substantial.[40]

Perry, however, misses the forest for the trees; the slaves were not employees who were paid for their daily toil. The master did not bargain with or hire slave labor; he owned it and used it up. If any slaves received cash "bonuses" at the end of each year, however substantial, as Peter Parish noted, those rewards were disproportionate to the quality and quantity of the work that they performed.[41] Finally, Perry claims that the master promised his slaves eventual freedom for years of service, loyalty, and hard labor.[42] But the typical slave in the ante-bellum South had virtually no chance of being freed by his captor. The absurdity of Perry's assertion becomes apparent if we consider (as did he) that in the year 1850 the manumission rate for slaves was only one to every 2,181 slaves.[43]

On the topic of American slavery, what American historians choose to focus upon is important and reveals much about their craft, their perceptions, and their biases. They should be concerned with presenting a true and accurate account of American slavery and promoting a better understanding of what white Southerners euphemistically called "the peculiar institution." Some are unable to do so because of their preoccupation with humanizing the slaveholder—presenting him in a more favorable light. Their apparent objective is to search out some goodness—any goodness—in the enormities. Although available records clearly show that masters, their overseers, and their slave drivers were disposed to inflicting severe pain and suffering on their slaves, certain influential American historians insist that brutal and inhuman slaveholders were exceptions to the general rule.

Democratic Sanity

Few American historians have raised serious questions regarding the mental competence of a people who would violently enslave thousands of human beings because of their skin color. Most presume the sanity of the perpetrators of the violence. Their tendency is to try to explain and justify the slaveholder's cruelty within the context of his society.[44] The psychologist Na'im Akbar elaborates on this phenomenon:

Traditional definitions of mental health in the Western world have been normative definitions. In the context of considerable uncertainty as to what constituted a normal human being, a kind of "democratic sanity" was established. This "democratic sanity" essentially applied the social political definition of majority rule to the definition of adequate human functioning. As a result . . . insane behavior is determined on the basis of the degree to which it deviates from the majority's behavior in a given context. . . . The consequence of such democratic sanity is that entire communities of raving inhuman lunatics have been adjudged sane and competent because the majority of people in that particular context either participated in the questionable behavior or refused to question the questionable behavior.[45]

Akbar suggests that one group of people's pertinacious oppression of another group merely because the former perceives a difference in the skin color of the latter has not been studied by the world's psychologists.[46] In fact, notable scholars who have studied racism are either reluctant—or find it a difficult challenge—to give serious consideration to its origins and the concomitant hostility.[47] They are content to study the peculiarly established patterns of racism.

Notes

1. Ulrich B. Phillips, *American Negro Slavery: A Survey of the Supply, Employment and Control of Negro Labor as Determined by the Plantation Regime* (1918; reprinted Baton Rouge: Louisiana State University Press, 1989).
2. Phillips contended that slave labor was unprofitable but that white control of blacks required that the American slavery regime survive.
3. Phillips, *American Negro Slavery*, 306, 343.
4. Samuel Eliot Morison and Henry Steele Commager, *The Growth of the American Republic*, rev. and enl. 4th ed. (New York: Oxford University Press, 1960), 537.
5. Kenneth M. Stampp, *The Peculiar Institution: Slavery in the Ante-Bellum South* (New York: Vintage Books, 1956), 148.
6. Stampp wrote, "Through religious instruction the bondsmen learned that slavery had a divine sanction, that insolence was as much an offense against God as against the temporal master." Stampp added that slaves "heard . . . that eternal salvation would be their reward for faithful service." Stampp, *The Peculiar Institution*, 158.
7. He wrote, "Some masters—often the ones with modest holdings—pursued a policy of kindness as far as possible . . . . The rewards and incentives took numerous forms . . . . The dollar may have been as important as kind words." Stampp, *The Peculiar Institution*, 164.
8. This is implicit in the following passage:

Most masters preferred the "persuasion doctrine" nevertheless. They would have been gratified if their slaves had willingly shown proper subordination and wholeheartedly responded to the *incentives* offered for efficient labor. They found, however, that some did not respond at all, and that others responded only intermittently. As a result, slaveholders were obliged to *sup-*

plement the lure of rewards for good behavior with the *threat* of punishment for bad.

Stampp, *The Peculiar Institution*, 171. (emphasis mine)

9. He noted that pro-slavery writers found cases of brutality extremely rare, travelers gave conflicting testimony, and abolitionists and ex-slaves insisted that cruelty was "more common than the defenders of the institution were willing to admit." Stampp, *The Peculiar Institution*, 181.

10. Stampp, *The Peculiar Institution*, 181.

11. Elkins wrote,

> In a system as tightly closed as the plantation . . . the slave's position of absolute dependency virtually compels him to see the authority figure as some how really "good." Indeed, all the evil in his life may flow from the man—but then also must anything of any value. Here is the seat of the only good he knows, and to maintain his psychic balance he must persuade himself that the good is in some way dominant. A threat to this illusion is thus in a real sense a threat to his very existence. . . . The most dramatic feature of this situation is the cruelty, which it involves, but the mechanism which inspires devotion is not the cruelty of the parent but rather the abnormal dependency of the child.

Stanley M. Elkins, *Slavery: A Problem in American Institutional and Intellectual Life* (Chicago: Univ. of Chicago Press, 1959), 129.

12. Gerald W. Mullin, *Flight and Rebellion: Slave Resistance in Eighteenth-Century Virginia* (New York: Oxford University Press, 1972).

13. Mullin wrote,

> The tone and phrases masters used while punishing slaves indicated they viewed slave rebelliousness in the context of the Fifth Commandment—Honor thy father and thy mother—assuming that both slaves and free had certain rights, duties and responsibilities toward one another. . . . A few sensational and well-publicized whippings should not obscure the view of the masters' sharply equivocal feelings about beating their 'people' . . . . Some whites became openly defensive and apologetic about physically 'correcting' slaves.

Mullin, *Flight and Rebellion*, 24.

14. Hence, for example, we find the economic historians Robert W. Fogel and Stanley L. Engerman asserting that whipping was "a fully acceptable form of punishment." Robert W. Fogel and Stanley L. Engerman, *Time on the Cross* (Boston: Little, Brown & Co., 1974), 144-46.

15. Mullin, *Flight and Rebellion*, 65.

16. John W. Blassingame, *The Slave Community: Plantation Life in the Ante-Bellum South*, rev. and enl. ed. (Cary, North Carolina: Oxford University Press, 1979).

17. George P. Rawick, *From Sundown to Sunup: The Making of the Black Community* (Westport, Conn.: Greenwood Publishing Co., 1972).

18. Lawrence W. Levine, *Black Culture and Black Consciousness* (New York: Oxford University Press, 1977).

19. E. Franklin Frazier, *The Negro Family in the United States* (Chicago: University of Chicago Press, 1939), 17.

20. Rawick, *From Sundown to Sunup*, Intro.

21. Levine, *Black Culture and Black Consciousness*, 45.

22. He wrote the following:

> However oppressive or dehumanizing the plantation was, the struggle for survival was not severe enough to crush all of the slave's creative instincts. Among elements of slave culture were: an emotional religion, folk songs and tales, dances and superstitions. Much of the slave's culture—language, customs, beliefs, and ceremonies—set him apart from his master. . . . The more his cultural forms differed from those of his master and the more they were immune from the control of whites, the more the slave gained personal autonomy and positive self-concepts.

Blassingame, *The Slave Community*, 105.

23. Fogel and Engerman, *Time on the Cross*, 144-49.

24. Fogel and Engerman wrote,

> Reliable data on the frequency of whipping is extremely sparse. . . . There is *nothing exceptional about the use of whipping* to enforce discipline among slaves until the beginning of the nineteenth century. It must be remembered that through centuries whipping was considered a fully acceptable form of punishment, not merely for criminals but also honest men or women who in some way shirked their duties. . . . To attribute the continuation of whipping in the South to the maliciousness of masters is naïve. Although some masters were brutal and even sadistic, most were not. . . . Such men worried about the proper role of whipping in a system of punishment and rewards. . . . Most accepted it, but recognized that to be effective whipping had to be used with restraint and in a coolly calculated manner. . . . While whipping was an integral part of the system of punishment and rewards, it was not the totality of the system. . . . To achieve the desired response slaveholders developed a wide-ranging system of rewards. . . . Occasionally, planters even devised elaborate schemes for profit sharing with their slaves.

Fogel and Engerman, *Time on the Cross*, 144-49. (emphasis mine)

25. Genovese contended, "The slaves objected not so much to punishment for disobeying rules, even when they thought the rules unfair, as to the arbitrariness, the caprice, the inhumanity that allowed one man to vent his passions on another." Eugene D. Genovese, *Roll Jordan Roll: The World the Slaves Made* (New York: Vintage Books, 1972), 67. This responsible parent concept is also present in the writings of the social scientists Robert W. Fogel and Stanley L. Engerman. They wrote, "Such men worried about the proper role of whipping in a system of punishment and rewards. . . . Most accepted it, but recognized that to be effective whipping had to be used with restraint and in a coolly calculated manner . . . ." Fogel and Engerman, *Time on the Cross*, 144-49.

26. James Oakes, *The Ruling Race: A History of American Slaveholders* (New York: Alfred A. Knopf, Inc., 1982), 4.

27. Genovese wrote the following:

This cruelty had to be and generally was condemned as barbarous, unchristian and unacceptable to civilized society but could only be recognized in its more extreme manifestations; cruelty, that is, could not easily be defined in the master-slave relationship. Outraged conscience aside, perceived cruelty seems to have been intolerable to society as whole primarily because it threatened a delicate fabric of implicit reciprocal duties, the acceptance of which by both masters and slaves alone could keep the system intact.

Genovese, *Roll, Jordan, Roll,* 72-73.

28. For example, a Georgia law of 1829 forbade teaching blacks to read, a Kentucky law of 1830 forbade them from attending school, and Alabama and Virginia laws of 1832 and a Missouri law of 1847 forbade teaching them to read or write. Claud Anderson, Ed.D, *Black Labor, White Wealth: The Search for Power and Economic Justice* (Edgewood, Md.: Duncan & Duncan, Inc., 1994), 225-26. Those laws, however, did not stop many slaves from actually learning to read and write. The historian John Hope Franklin noted, "In the nineteenth century Negroes in the Southern states had to content themselves, for the most part, with clandestine schools and private teachers." John Hope Franklin and Alfred A. Moss, Jr., *From Slavery to Freedom,* 6th ed. (New York: Alfred A. Knopf, Inc., 1988), 92.

29. Genovese, *Roll, Jordan, Roll,* 39.

30. Genovese, *Roll, Jordan, Roll,* 39.

31. Rhett S. Jones, "Structural Isolation, Race and Cruelty in the New World," *Third World Review* 4, no. 2 (Fall 1978): 35.

32. Elkins, *Slavery: A Problem in American Institutional and Intellectual Life,* 58.

33. Peter J. Parish, *Slavery: History and Historians* (New York: Harper & Row Publishers, 1989), 1-9.

34. Parish, *Slavery: History and Historians,* 23-24.

35. He wrote the following:

Clearly, the use of rewards and incentives, even if widespread, would not itself prove that coercion was unimportant in making slaves work hard. It is surely in the nature of a slave system that force, or the threat of force, is fundamental and all other methods are secondary. Two basic conditions which set the pattern of slave control were the fact or the threat of punishment (whether by whipping or other means) and the generally poor prospects of successful and permanent escape.

Parish, *Slavery: History and Historians,* 34-35.

36. John C. Perry, *Myths & Realities of American Slavery* (Shippensburg, Pa.: Burd Street Press, 2002), 135-36.

37. Franklin and Moss, *From Slavery to Freedom,* 119-20.

38. Norman Y. Yetman, ed., *Voices from Slavery: 100 Authentic Slave Narratives* (Toronto: General Publishing Company, Ltd., 2000), 77.

39. For example, the North Carolina ex-slave W.L. Post made the following comment:

I remember how they kill one nigger whippin' him with a bullwhip. Many poor nigger nearly killed with the bullwhip. But this one die. He was a stubborn Negro and didn't do as much work as his massa thought he ought to. He been lashed lot before. So they take him to the whippin' post, and then they strip his clothes off and then the man stand off and cut him with the whip. His back was cut all to pieces. The cuts about a half inch apart. Then after they whip him they tie him down and put salt on him. Then after he lie in the sun awhile they whip him agin. But when they finish with he, he was dead.

Yetman, *Voices from Slavery*, 37.
> 40. Perry, *Myths & Realities of American Slavery*, 136.
> 41. Parish, Slavery: *Historians and History*, 38.
> 42. Perry wrote the following:

Perhaps the most popular reward was cash. Usually cash was given for short-term performance, but some slave owners developed the forerunner of a modern corporate bonus plan by giving slaves a cash 'bonus,' often at the end of the year. Some cash bonus amounts paid to slaves were quite substantial . . . . Perhaps the ultimate reward was the promise of eventual freedom for years of service, loyalty and hard work.

Perry, *Myths & Realities of American Slavery*, 136-37.
> 43. Perry, *Myths & Realities of American Slavery*, 137;   Joseph Kennedy, ed., *Population of the United States in 1860; Compiled from the Original Returns of the Eighth Census, Under the Direction of the Secretary of the Interior* (Washington, D.C., 1864), xv.
> 44. The historian Gerald Mullin, for example, argued, "Byrd's brutal humiliation of Eugene [his slave] is partially understandable in the context of his society—one which legitimized such forms of violence and judicial torture." Mullin, *Flight and Rebellion*, 66.
> 45. Na'im Akbar, "Mental Disorder among African-Americans," *Black Books Bulletin* 7, no. 2 (1981): 19.
> 46. Akbar, "Mental Disorder," 19.
> 47. I refer to Sidney Mintz, Eric Williams, Locksley Edmundson, Oscar and Mary Handlin, Carl Degler, George Fredrickson, and Winthrop Jordan.

CHAPTER TWO

A Monopoly of Violence in the Slaveholder's Hands

"If men's superiority over the brute creation consists only in his reasoning powers and rationality of mind, his various methods of practicing violence toward his fellow creatures has in many cases placed him on a level with, and sometimes below, many species of the quadruped race."

—WILLIAM WHIPPER,
"An Address on Non-resistance to Offensive Aggression,"
The Colored American, 16 September 1837

Some American slavery historians, Ulrich B. Phillips to name one, believed that the master-slave relationship was built upon a reciprocal benevolent concern for each party's interest or well-being—something more morally acceptable than a monopoly of violence in the slaveholder's hands.[1] The relationship, however, was one created and maintained through torture. The slave was a captive. If he escaped, where might his hideout be for protection? He might have found temporary refuge in the woods, but slave resistance was vigorously suppressed, not just by the individual power of violence in the slaveowner's hands, but by a social and collective community power that had nothing to do with the master's so-called paternalistic concern for the well-being of his slaves. Thus, the absence of widespread insurrection among enslaved black people in the ante-bellum South was not due to an abnormal dependency on their part, nor attributed to a delicate fabric of implicit reciprocal duties which was accepted by both slaveholders and slaves. Nor can we credit it to a calculated and balanced system of torture and rewards.

This is not to suggest that all slaveholders subjected their slaves to physically injurious treatment. Some masters who did not believe in whipping their rebellious slaves simply "put them in their pocket"—selling and separating them from their loved ones.[2] Nevertheless, as the ex-slave Charles Ball noted, humane slaveholders were "like angels' visits—few and far between."[3]

Only through a clearer understanding of the coercive apparatuses developed in the Old South will we better understand the absence of widespread insurrection. In the United States, slaveowners violently forced Africans into what the historian Angela Y. Davis called "a patently 'unnatural' subjugation." She elaborated: "If the slaveholders had not maintained an absolute monopoly of violence, if they had not been able to rely on large numbers of their fellow white men . . . to assist them in their terrorist machinations, slavery would have been far less feasible than it actually proved to be."[4] Many of the ex-slave interviews recorded in the 1930s and virtually all of the slave narratives published before the American Civil War document the violence slaveholders used to suppress slave resistance.[5] Not only do these acts of torture appear frequently in the slave narratives, they seem central to slave life.[6]

We may divide the forms of repression used by the slaveholding class to subjugate black slaves during the ante-bellum period into three major categories: torture on the plantations, legally-sanctioned repression, and repression by the omnipresent slave patrols surrounding the plantations.

Torture on the Plantations

The first form of repression was the torture of slaves on the plantations, the method of which was left totally to the discretion of the slaveholders. They employed a variety of means to torture their slaves. The ex-slave William Wells Brown noted that one of his masters would tie him up in a smoke-house and whip him. After this, he would cause a fire to be made and "smoke" him. This was called "Virginia Play."[7] In the following passage, Charles Ball provides an account of a sadistic instance in which a slaveholder took a large grey tom-cat, placed it upon the bare back of a prostrate black man, and forcibly dragged the cat by the tail from the man's shoulder, down his back, and along his bare thighs:

> The cat sunk his nails into the flesh and tore off pieces of skin with his teeth. The man roared with the pain of this punishment. . . . This was the most excruciating punishment that I ever saw inflicted on black people, and . . . it is very dangerous; for the claws of the cat are poisonous, and the wounds made by them are very subject to inflammation.[8]

Another form of torture was the sweatbox. The South Carolina ex-slave Prince Smith told us that the box was made the height of the slave and no larger, just large enough so he would not have to squeeze in. The slaveholder would force his slave to get in the box and he would then nail it shut. In the summer, he would place the box in the hot sun; in the winter, he would put it in the coldest dampest place.[9] Mary Ella Grandberry, a former slave from Alabama, referred to a similar form of torture as the "nigger box." The master drilled air holes into the box to keep his slave from suffocating. Grandberry said, "Iffen you had done a bigger 'nough thing you was kept in de 'nigger box' for months at a time, and when you got out you was nothing but skin and bones and scarcely able to walk."[10] Writing between 1824 and 1835, the traveler Nehemiah Caulkins recorded that he saw another slave who was buried up to his chin, his arms being secured down by his sides, and was kept in this position four or five days.[11] An ex-slave from Mississippi, Sarah Ross, recalled that slaveholders found no kind of torture too cruel or severe to inflict upon their slaves. She said, "Frequently, the thighs of the male slaves were gashed with a saw and salt put in the wound . . . ."[12]

The Cat-O'-Nine-Tails

The most frequent form of torture was the lash,[13] commonly referred to by ex-slaves as the "cat-o'-nine tails"—meaning that every lash produced nine licks. The cat-o'-nine tails was a whip of nine leather straps attached to a stick. On some, the leather straps were braided; on others, they were perforated, so that everywhere the hole in the strap came in contact with the flesh it would leave a blister. Often after a severe whipping, typically performed by an overseer or slave driver, the slave's raw and open wounds would be treated to water containing salt. The slaveholders called this treatment the salt water cure, but it cured nothing. It merely aggravated the slave's pain and made it longer-lasting.[14]

John Perry found little solid historical data on whippings to examine.[15] Nonetheless, the revered historian John Hope Franklin aptly noted that "efforts at statistical computation of whippings are pointless if not ridiculous." He charged that in an effort to get work out of his slaves, the master frequently used the bullwhip, almost no slaveholders disclaimed whipping as an effective form of torture, and the excessive use of the lash was one of the most egregious abuses of the American slavery regime.[16]

Information gathered from the slave narratives reveals that no matter how good or useful the slave was, he seldom escaped the lash. The Texas ex-slave Katie Darling remembered that when a slave did anything the master would bullwhip him. She said, "He'd whip the man for half doin' the plowin' or hoein', but if they done it right he'd find something else to whip them for."[17] The former slave Henry Bibb's master would keep no overseer on his plantation that neglected to perform the duty every morning. "I have heard him say," wrote Bibb, "that he was no better pleased than when he could hear . . . the sound of the driver's lash among the toiling slaves."[18] Dennis Simms, an ex-slave from Maryland, recalled as well that slaves had to "toe the mark or be flogged with a rawhide whip," and almost everyday on the plantation there were from two to ten thrashings given to disobedient black slaves.[19] The ninety-year-old North Carolina ex-slave Andrew Boone describes in graphic detail how the slaveholders used the cat-o'-nine tails to torture him and other slaves:

I saw a lot of slaves whupped and I was whupped myself. Dey whupped me with de cat-o'-nine-tails. It had nine lashes on it. Some of the slaves was whupped with a cobbin paddle. Dey had forty holes in 'em an' when you was buckled to a barrel dey hit your naked flesh wid de paddle an' everywhere dere was a hole in the paddle it drawed a blister. When the whuppin' with de paddle was over, dey took the cat-o'-nine-tails and busted de blisters. By dis time de blood sometimes would be runnin' down dere heels. Den de next thing was a wash in salt water strong enough to hold up an egg. Slaves was punished dat way for runnin' away an' such.[20]

Over ninety years old at the time of his interview, Henry Johnson, a former slave from Virginia, recalled vivid memories of the paddle and the lash. He said,

Slaves have been stripped naked and lashed, often to death. Dey would be left strapped after from twenty-five to fifty lashes every two or three hours to stand there all night. De next day, de overseer would be back with a heavy paddle full of holes that had been dipped in boiling water and beat until de whole body was full of blisters. Den he'd take a cat-and-nine-tails dipped in hot salt water to draw out de bruised blood and would open every one of those blisters with dat. If de slave did not die from dat torture, he would be unfastened from the whipping post, and made to go to de field just as he was. Oftentimes he would die shortly after.[21]

Slaves did not have to commit infractions to be whipped. Barney Stone, a former slave from Kentucky, said that he saw his mother beaten mercilessly by his master for no good reason.[22] The Oklahoma ex-slave John White, 121 years old when interviewed, exclaimed, "Master Presley used his whip all the time, reason or no reason, and I got scars to remember by!"[23] The Arkansas ex-slave J. T. Tims similarly told us, "When Old Miss was whipping me, I asked her what she was whipping me for, and she said 'Nothin', 'cause you're mine, and I can whip you if I want to.'"[24] A former slave from Missouri, Jane Simpson recalled as well that her mistress whipped her when she had done nothing.[25] Thus, slaveholders whipped blacks in the ante-bellum South not only for running away or lagging behind in their labor. It was not enough that the master controlled the labor of his slaves. Psycho-political motives also fueled the slaveowner's acts of cruelty. His objectives were two-fold: convince black people that they are innately inferior—less human, and impress upon them a sense of his enormous power.

Certain slaveholders and slave drivers whipped obedient slaves to vent anger; others found whipping them a source of perverse gratification. J. T. Tims recalled that his mistress whipped him because she was "just mad that day," and he was around, so she took it out on him.[26] Jane Simpson said that if her mistress "got mad about something, just anything at all," she would whip her "just to satisfy her spite feeling."[27] Touring the rice and sugar plantations of the Deep South in 1830, the traveler Simon Ansley Ferrall noted that it was "a fact, well known to persons who have visited slave countries," that torture was "more frequently inflicted to gratify the private pique or caprice of the [slave] driver, than for crime or neglect of duty."[28]

Slaveholders, slave drivers, and overseers whipped obedient slaves because they commanded unlimited power to do it. They were also mindful that frequent use of violence instilled fear in their slaves, and that was essential to securing total control. "We have to rely more and more on the power of fear," wrote one slaveholder. "We are determined to continue as masters," he noted, "and to do so we have to draw the reign tighter and tighter day by day to be assured that we hold them in complete check."[29]

Notes

1. Consider, for example, the following comments of Ulrich B. Phillips:

> The general regime was in fact shaped by mutual requirements, concessions and understandings, producing reciprocal codes of conventional morality. Masters of the standard type . . . avoided cruel, vindictive and captious punishments, and endeavored to inspire effort through affection rather than through fear; and they were content with achieving quite moderate industrial results. In short their despotism, so far as it might properly be so called was benevolent in intent and on the whole beneficial in effect.

Ulrich B. Phillips, *American Negro Slavery: A Survey of the Supply, Employment and Control of Negro Labor as Determined by the Plantation Regime* (1918; reprinted Baton Rouge: Louisiana State University Press, 1989), 327-28.

2. According to the North Carolina ex-slave Sarah Debro, "put them in their pocket" meant that the masters would sell the slaves and put the proceeds from the sale in their pocket. Norman Y. Yetman, ed., *Voices from Slavery: 100 Authentic Slave Narratives* (Toronto: General Publishing Company, Ltd., 2000), 98.

3. Charles Ball, *Slavery in the United States: A Narrative of the Life and Adventures of Charles Ball, a Black Man, Who Lived Forty Years in Maryland, South Carolina and Georgia, as a Slave* (Lewistown, Pa.: J. W. Shugert, 1836), 77.

4. Angela Davis, "Reflections on the Black Woman's Role in the Community of Slaves," *Black Scholar* 3, no. 4 (December 1971): 6.

5. The historian John C. Perry dismisses virtually all of the nearly one hundred former slave autobiographies written before the Civil War as not a "good source of slave detail" because he thinks they were "typically financed and strongly edited by the abolitionists." In fact, Perry criticizes John Blassingame's *Slave Community* for its "frequent" use of slave autobiographies, which he calls "biased" and "inaccurate." He decides to make the credibility determination for us and, predictably, finds none of those ex-slaves credible. In Perry's view, they were incapable of providing true and accurate first-hand accounts of their American experiences as slaves. John C. Perry, *Myths & Realities of American Slavery* (Shippensburg, Pa.: Burd Street Press, 2002), 71-73, 241. There is value, however, in all sources. As the ex-slave Frederick Douglass noted in a letter to his editor on July 2, 1855, "Any facts, either from slaves, slavehold-

ers, or by-standers, calculated to enlighten the public mind, by revealing the true nature, character, and tendency of the slave system, are in order, and can scarcely be innocently withheld." Frederick Douglass, *My Bondage and My Freedom* (Chicago: Johnson Publishing Co., 1970), 2.

6. George P. Rawick, *From Sundown to Sunup: The Making of the Black Community* (Westport, Conn.: Greenwood Publishing Company, 1972), 5.

7. William Wells Brown, *Narrative of William Wells Brown* (Boston, 1847), 48-51.

8. Ball, *Slavery in the United States,* 286.

9. George P. Rawick, ed., *The American Slave: A Composite Autobiography,* 41 vols. (Westport, Conn.: Greenwood Publishing Co., 1972), South Carolina, part 4, 117.

10. Yetman, *Voices from Slavery,* 145.

11. Rev. Theodore D. Weld et al, ed., *Slavery as It Is: Testimony of a Thousand Witnesses* (New York: American Anti-Slavery Society, 1839), 15.

12. *Born in Slavery: Slave Narratives from the Federal Writers' Project, 1936-1938,* (Wash., D.C.: Library of Congress, 2001), Florida Narratives, vol. 3, 168. <http://memory.loc.gov/ammem/snhtml> (15 April 2006).

13. The historian Nathan Irvin Huggins wrote, "There was hardly a slave who did not as an adult suffer the lash." Nathan Irvin Huggins, *Black Odyssey: The Afro-American Ordeal in Slavery* (New York: Pantheon Books, 1977), 122.

14. *Born in Slavery: Slave Narratives from the Federal Writers' Project,* Florida Narratives, vol. 3, 67.

15. Perry, *Myths & Realities of American Slavery,* 135.

16. John Hope Franklin and Alfred A. Moss, Jr., *From Slavery to Freedom* (New York: Alfred A. Knopf, Inc., 1988), 119.

17. Yetman, *Voices from Slavery,* 70.

18. Henry Bibb, *Narrative of the Life and Adventures of Henry Bibb, An American Slave* (New York, 1849), 286.

19. Rawick, *The American Slave,* Maryland, 60.

20. Yetman, *Voices from Slavery,* 33-34; *Born in Slavery: Slave Narratives from the Federal Writers' Project,* North Carolina Narratives, vol. 11, part 1, 134.

21. *Born in Slavery: Slave Narratives from the Federal Writers' Project,* Missouri Narratives, vol. 10, 206-7.

22. *Born in Slavery: Slave Narratives from the Federal Writers' Project,* Indiana Narratives, vol. 5, 187.

23. Yetman, *Voices from Slavery,* 307.

24. Yetman, *Voices from Slavery,* 303.

25. Yetman, *Voices from Slavery,* 279.

26. Yetman, *Voices from Slavery,* 303.

27. Yetman, *Voices from Slavery,* 279.

28. Simon Ansley Ferrall, *Ramble of Six Thousand Miles Through the United States of America* (London: E. Wilson, Publisher, 1832), 196.

29. *De Bow's Review* VII (1849): 498.

CHAPTER THREE

The Slaves' Undying Faith in God

"Faith is the flip side of fear."

—SUSAN TAYLOR,
1988

When it came to their slaves, the slaveholders had two approaches to the Bible: keep it away from them and try to use it as a weapon of indoctrination. The First Amendment to the United States Constitution in part states, "Congress shall make no law respecting an establishment of religion, or prohibiting the free exercise thereof."[1] With that in mind, some of us might find a difficulty in accepting the following premise: in the United States of America—a country founded upon the principle of religious freedom—one group of people forcibly prevented another group from worshipping God. But the First Amendment did not undertake to protect even the religious liberty of white people against the action of their respective state governments,[2] and in an effort to control the soul and break the independent religious spirit of Africans, the slaveholders of the ante-bellum South were determined to keep them ignorant of the Bible. Unless it promoted his self-interest, the master saw the danger inherent in his slaves' worship of God.[3] The Arkansas ex-slave Lucretia Alexander recalled always hearing the same sermon from a Baptist preacher. She said,

> The preacher came to preach to [the slaves] in their quarters. He'd just say, "Serve your masters. Don't steal your master's turkey. Don't steal your master's chickens. Don't steal your master's hogs. Don't steal your master's meat. Do whatsomeever your master tell you to do." Same old thing all de time.[4]

Interviewed in 1936, the 108-year-old Florida ex-slave "Father" Charles Coates recalled as well a white minister instructing him not to steal, lie, or run away, and to "be sure and git all dem weeds outen dat corn in de field and your master will think a heap of you."[5] Coates remembered nothing else the preacher told him. He learned more about God outside of the church. A former slave from Georgia, Hannah Austin, said that the slaves on her plantation seldom heard a true religious sermon; instead, they were instructed to obey their masters and mistresses.[6]

Fearful of their owners, some black ministers gave sermons that were no different from those of the white preachers. John White told us that an old black preacher on his plantation just talked about the master and the mistress, how the slaves must obey around the plantation, and "how white folks know what is good for the slaves." The black minister said nothing about obeying God and working for him. White exclaimed, "I reckon the old preacher was worrying more about the bullwhip than he was the Bible, else he say something about the Lord!"[7]

The anti-slavery advocate Reverend William Goodell explained that the master's claim on his slave extended to the slave's soul as well as his body; otherwise, the body could not have been held and controlled.[8] Through religious instruction, the slaveholders tried to convince their slaves that slavery enjoyed divine sanction—it was commanded by the Bible—and if the slaves led a life of loyal servitude, eternal salvation would be their reward. The slaves, however, were not convinced. William Ward, a 105-year-old ex-slave from Georgia, said, "None of the slaves believed this, although they pretended to believe because of the presence of the white overseer."[9] Most slaves realized that their masters had misrepresented and perverted the word of God. Reverend Goodell hardly could have faulted them for their skepticism. In 1853, he wrote, "It is no discredit to the slaves that they have little or no desire to hear religious harangues from their oppressors, or that they loathe the instructions of ministers who preach the righteousness of slaveholding."[10]

The English poet and philosopher Samuel Taylor Coleridge noted, "By a principle essential to Christianity, a person is eternally differenced from a thing; so that the idea of a human being, necessarily excludes the idea of property in that being."[11] Coleridge revealed the contradiction of professing to be a Christian and owning slaves. Evangelical Protestantism, a religious faith followed by many slaveholders, promoted egalitarianism and explicitly rejected materialism. If those masters were not mindful that their faith was clearly at odds with slaveholding—the sole purpose of which was to amass wealth at the expense of brutally dehumanizing their captives—the slaves' dogged refusal to succumb to their owners' use of Christianity as a weapon of indoctrination was an enduring reminder to those slaveholders of that contradiction.[12]

The slave suffered physically, but compared to his captor he believed that he was the more righteous, albeit practically speaking, powerless one. He was a spiritual being, and his spiritually-grounded resistance to slavery his master feared. In fact, the North Carolina ex-slave W. L. Post said, "White folks feared for niggers to get any religion."[13] Slaveholders were apprehensive of permitting their slaves to have unsupervised religious instruction because they were concerned that it would enlighten them.[14] It would teach them that all human beings were created equal in the eyes of God, and that any system of governance that supported the enslavement and dehumanization of a people because of the color of their skin was evil, immoral, and un-Christian.

Some masters also worried that if the slaves were left alone to choose their own modes and forms of religious worship, it might lead to insubordination—or worse—to insurrection. For surely most members of the slaveholding class knew that over fifty of their own people were killed in Southhampton County, Virginia during the Nat Turner Insurrection of August 21-23, 1831. Moreover, they understood that Nat Turner himself, free of fear, believed that he was commanded by God to "give a death blow" to those intent on protecting and preserving an evil and immoral American slavery regime.[15]

As far as the slaveholding class was concerned, black religious freedom was incompatible with slavery.[16] But the slaves' undying faith in God was one no captor could take away. The 100-year-old Alabama ex-slave Delia Garlic recalled that trusting in the Lord was the only hope of the slaves in those days. She said, "Us just prayed for strength to endure it to de end."[17] Some slaves would steal away and attend night prayer meetings, though those meetings were prohibited by slave codes.[18] They appreciated the dangers of attending those religious services. Charlotte Martin, a former slave from Florida, told us that her master whipped her oldest brother to death for taking part in a secret night prayer meeting, and that the cruel act halted further clandestine religious services.[19]

Silas Jackson also remembered a master who murdered his slave for praying. The slaveholder overheard a slave named Zeek praying in his cabin one night. Zeek asked God to change his master's heart and to deliver him from slavery so that he might enjoy freedom. He disappeared before sunrise, never to be seen again. Although the slaves claimed they could still hear Zeek praying down by the swamp on certain nights of the month, on his death bed, his master confessed to a Baptist minister that he had killed him for praying. The dying slaveholder foretold that he himself was going to hell because of it.[20]

Other slaves realized that slave patrols were predisposed to disrupt religious gatherings. W. L. Post said, "Sometimes the patterrollers catch us and beat us good but that didn't keep us from trying." He recalled memories of his mother singing and praying to God to deliver them from bondage.[21] The Alabama ex-slave Mingo White remembered as well that after the slaves completed their day's work, they would lock themselves in their cabins—praying to the Lord to free them like he did the children of Israel.[22]

Several former slaves gave various accounts of their practice of using a large empty pot to keep the slave patrols and slaveholders from overhearing their singing and praying. The Virginia ex-slave Minnie Fulkes, for example, said that her mother informed her that the slaves "use to have meetings an' sing and pray an' th' ol' paddy rollers would hear dem, so to keep th' sound from goin' out, slaves would put a great big iron pot at the door." Fulkes added, "Sometimes dey would fer git to put the ol' pot dar an' the paddy rollers would come an' horse whip every las' one of 'em, jes cause poor souls wuz praying to God to free 'em from dat awful bondage."[23] North Carolina and Arkansas ex-slaves Henry Bobbitt and Cyrus Bellus recalled that other slaves would turn the kettles in their cabins bottom up in the belief that their masters would not overhear their singing and praying.[24] The Arkansas ex-slave Rachel Fairley's mother told her that before praying for freedom she put her head under a large cooking pot.[25]

Cooking pot or not, some slaveholders severely whipped slaves whom they caught praying. Mingo White commented on an incident involving an old slave named Ned White. He said that the following happened to Ned when his master caught him praying:

> De drivers took him the next day and carried him to the pegs, what was four stakes drove in de ground. Ned was made to pull off everything but his pants and lay on his stomach between the pegs whilst somebody strapped his legs and arms to de pegs. Den dey whipped him till de blood run from him like he was a hog. Dey made all of the hands come and see it, and dey said us get the same thing if us was catched. Dey don't allow a man to whip a horse like dey whipped us in dem days.[26]

Minnie Fulkes also recollected that impious masters would beat and whip their slaves severely to prevent them from serving the Lord. She said,

> Dey would come in and start whippin' an' beatin' the slaves unmerciful. All dis wuz done to keep yo' from servin' God an' do you know some of dem devils was mean an' sinful 'nough to say, "Ef I ketch you here agin servin' God I'll beat you. You haven't time to serve God. We bought you here to serve us."

Convinced that eventually those slaveholders would have to answer to the Lord for their immoral transgressions, Minnie Fulkes predicted, "God's gwine 'rod dem wicket marsters. Ef hit 'taint 'em what gits hit, hits gonna fall on deir chillun."[27]

Celestia Avery remembered the cruel treatment her grandmother Sylvia Heard received when she prayed. She said,

> Every morning my grandmother would pray and old man Heard despised to hear anyone pray saying that they were only doing so that they might become free niggers. Just as sure as the sun would rise, she would get a whipping; but this did not stop her prayers every morning before day.[28]

In spite of the master's torture of Celestia Avery's grandmother, she remained undaunted. Notwithstanding her owner's enormous power, the whippings did not stop her daily prayers because this spiritual woman's strong faith and trust in God—her true master—gave her the strength, courage, and will to endure. With the Lord by her side, Sylvia Heard conquered her fear; as for her captor, she believed that his judgment day was near.

Notes

1. U.S. Const., Amendment 1.

2. Thomas M. Cooley, LL.D., *The General Principles of Constitutional Law in the United States of America* (Boston: Little Brown & Company, 1898), 224.

3. As one means of attempting to secure obedience, slaveholders used religious instruction. They quoted verses from the Bible, instructing their slaves to "obey your earthly masters with respect and fear, and sincerity of heart, just as you would obey Christ" and "serve wholeheartedly, as if you were serving the Lord, not men." Ephesians 6:5-9.

4. Norman Y. Yetman, ed., *Voices from Slavery: 100 Authentic Slave Narratives* (Toronto: General Publishing Company, Ltd., 2000), 12-13.

5. *Born in Slavery: Slave Narratives from the Federal Writers' Project, 1936-1938* (Wash., D.C.: Library of Congress, 2001), Florida Narratives, vol. 3, 68. <http://memory.loc.gov/ammem/snhtml> (15 April 2006).

6. *Born in Slavery: Slave Narratives from the Federal Writers' Project*, Georgia Narratives, vol. 4, part 1, 20.

7. *Born in Slavery: Slave Narratives from the Federal Writers' Project*, Oklahoma Narratives, vol. 13, 325.

8. William Goodell, *The American Slave Code in Theory and Practice: Its Distinctive Features Shown by Its Statutes, Judicial Decisions, and Illustrative Facts* (New York: American and Foreign Anti-Slavery Society, 1853) pt. 1, ch. 12, 254.

9. *Born in Slavery: Slave Narratives from the Federal Writers' Project*, Georgia Narratives, vol. 4, part 4, 129.

10. Goodell, *The American Slave Code*, pt. 2, ch. 7, 331.

11. Frederick Douglas, *My Bondage and My Freedom* (Chicago: Johnson Publishing Co., 1970), iii.

12. Oakes, *The Ruling Race*, 107.

13. Yetman, *Voices from Slavery*, 37.

14. On November 2, 1838, it was reported in the *Greenville Mountaineer*, a South Carolina newspaper of the time, that a document signed by James S. Pope and 352 other South Carolinians argued at length the incompatibility of slavery with the "mental improvement and religious instruction" of slaves. As summarized, the argument was that mental improvement through religious instruction would enlighten black people and render their condition "more unhappy and intolerable." Goodell, *The American Slave Code*, pt. 2, ch. 7, 336-337.

15. William F. Cheek, *Black Resistance before the Civil War* (Beverly Hills, Calif.: Glencoe Press, 1970), 122. Although Nat Turner's execution in Jerusalem, Virginia on November 11, 1831 was inevitable, God's warrior secured his place in American history.

16. Goodell, *The American Slave Code*, pt. 2, ch. 7, 336-337.

17. Yetman, *Voices from Slavery*, 134.

18. Perhaps because of the Nat Turner Insurrection of 1831, the Virginia Legislature that year passed a law prohibiting free black people from preaching or conducting religious services, day or night, and prohibiting slaves and free blacks from attending those religious services. The law also prohibited slaves from listening to white preachers at night. The penalty for violating that law was up to 39 lashes. Mississippi had a similar law. Goodell, *The American Slave Code*, pt. 2, ch. 7, 331-332. Among the ordinances passed by the City of Augusta, Georgia on February 7, 1862 was Section forty-seven, concerning any meeting of slaves or free persons of color for public worship or religious instruction. That section in pertinent part provided the following:

> No meeting of slaves or free persons of color for the purpose of [public worship or religious instruction] shall continue at any time later than 10:30 at night. . . . All slaves or free persons of color attending such meetings, after that hour, shall be arrested, and punished, under the Section, whether with or without tickets from their owners. . . . Every offense against this Section shall be punished by whipping, not exceeding 39 lashes, or fined not exceeding $50.00.

Born in Slavery: Slave Narratives from the Federal Writers' Project, Georgia Narratives, vol. 4, part 4, 318-19.

19. *Born in Slavery: Slave Narratives from the Federal Writers' Project*, Florida Narratives, vol. 3, 166.

20. The facts are taken from the testimony of the Virginia ex-slave Silas Jackson. Yetman, *Voices from Slavery*, 177.

21. Yetman, *Voices from Slavery*, 37.

22. Yetman, *Voices from Slavery*, 312.

23. *Born in Slavery: Slave Narratives from the Federal Writers' Project*, Virginia Narratives, vol. 17, 11-12.

24. *Born in Slavery: Slave Narratives from the Federal Writers' Project*, North Carolina Narratives, vol. 11, part 1, 121; Arkansas Narratives, vol. 2, part 1, 142.

25. *Born in Slavery: Slave Narratives from the Federal Writers' Project*, Arkansas Narratives, vol. 2, part 2, 258.

26. Yetman, *Voices from Slavery*, 312.

27. *Born in Slavery: Slave Narratives from the Federal Writers' Project*, Virginia Narratives, vol. 17, 12.

28. *Born in Slavery: Slave Narratives from the Federal Writers' Project*, Georgia Narratives, vol. 4, part 1, 24.

CHAPTER FOUR

The Torture of Black Women and Children

Black women were as powerless, vulnerable, and fearful as black men in-asmuch as they were also tortured. Nancy Boudry, a former slave from Georgia, said, "Dey whup me, dey whup me bad, pull de clothes off the wais'—my master did it."[1] Slaveholders whipped female slave-cooks almost to death for such minor omissions and oversights as forgetting to put onions in the stew and burning the bread.[2] Born Isabella Baumfree, the ex-slave and human rights advocate Sojourner Truth remembered one slave-woman whom her master whipped until "the flesh was lacerated, and blood streaming from her wounds—and the scars remain to present day to testify to the fact." "And now," noted Truth, "when I hear 'em tell of whipping women on the bare flesh, it makes my flesh crawl, and my hair rise on my head."[3]

Southern white women also whipped black women sadistically and bru-tally.[4] In his autobiography, the former slave James L. Smith wrote about Miss Mitchell, a heartless mistress who whipped a slave-woman named Jenny in a very cruel manner. "She would apply a rawhide to her back until she had ex-hausted her own strength," wrote Smith. She would rest for a few minutes while keeping Jenny standing, and "after resting her weary arms, she com-menced again. Thus, whipped and rested, until she had applied fifty blows upon her suffering back." Mistress Mitchell then sent Jenny back to the kitchen to work with her back sore and bleeding.[5] Sojourner Truth noted one mistress of high social standing who "was actually beating in the skull of a slave-woman called Tabby; and not content with that, had her tied up and whipped after her skull was broken." This victim of unrestrained physical cru-elty died hanging to the bedstead.[6]

Slave-parents could not shield their children from the wrath of the mis-tress. The ninety-one-year-old Texas ex-slave Mary Armstrong was owned by an evil mistress called "Old Polly" Cleveland. Old Polly, in her opinion, was one of the "meanest white folks whatever lived." Mary Armstrong said,

> Old Polly, she was a Polly devil if there ever was one, and she whipped my little sister what was only nine months old and jes' a baby, to death. She come and took the diaper offen my little sister and whipped till the blood jes' ran—jes' 'cause she cry like all babies do, and it kilt my sister.[7]

Pregnancy and motherhood, though essential to the prosperity of the American slavery regime, provided no shelter under which the pregnant or nursing bondswoman could hide to avoid torture. "Father" Charles Coates said that the pregnant slave received no more leniency than did the bondsman.[8] Like the male slave, she typically was required to work from sunup-to-sundown—a twelve-to-thirteen-hour workday, six days a week. On the cotton plantations in the ante-bellum South, each slave generally was expected to pick at least 150 pounds of cotton a day.[9] Bondsmen and bondswomen suffered equally under the repressive American slavery regime because the slaveholder demanded the same of both.

Under constant supervision, pregnant slave-women performed long, fatiguing labor. In his conversation with James G. Birney in 1834, the slaveholder and Kentucky U.S. Senator Henry Clay described an overseer in Louisiana who worked his hands so closely that one bondswoman gave birth to a child while engaged in the labors of the field.[10] Sam and Louisa "Nor" Everett, ex-slaves from Norfolk, Virginia, told us as well that expectant slave-mothers toiled in the fields until they felt their labor pains, and it was not uncommon for their babies to be born in the fields.[11]

Expectant slave-mothers worked hard in those fields under the threat of bodily harm.[12] Indeed, many slaveholders saw nothing morally repugnant about torturing pregnant slaves who could not keep up with other field hands. Sarah Ross recalled that certain masters would instruct their overseers to torture them by whipping them about the shoulders, not so much in pity as for protection of the slaveholders' unborn property interests.[13] According to her granddaughter, one slave-woman who was "in the family way" was seized, stripped, tied to a "young sapling," and whipped "so brutally that her body was raw all over."[14] These violent acts against expectant and nursing slave-mothers were not infrequent. The ex-slave Moses Grandy provides a detailed account of how the overseer on his plantation tortured slave-mothers with nursing babies and others who were pregnant:

> Those women who had suckling children suffer much from their breasts becoming full of milk, the infants being left at home; they therefore could not keep up with the other hands. I have seen the overseer beat them with rawhide, so the blood and milk flew mingled from their breasts. A woman who gives offense in the field, and is large in the family way, is compelled to

lie down over a hole made to receive the corpulency, and is flogged with a whip, or beat with a paddle, which has holes in it; at every hole comes a blister. One of my sisters was so severely punished in this way that labor was brought on, and the child was born in the field.[15]

One overseer actually tortured a pregnant slave to death. The Mississippi ex-slave Clara C. Young saw him whip her pregnant cousin until she bled. "She was just seventeen years old and was in de family way for de first time and couldn't work as hard as de rest," stated Young. Her pregnant cousin died the following morning from the whipping.[16]

Notes

1. *Born in Slavery: Slave Narratives from the Federal Writers' Project, 1936-1938* (Wash., D.C.: Library of Congress, 2001), Georgia Narratives, vol. 4, part 1, 113-14. <http://memory.loc.gov/ammem/snhtml> (15 April 2006).

2. *Born in Slavery: Slave Narratives from the Federal Writers' Project,* Kentucky Narratives, vol. 7, 67; Norman Y. Yetman, ed., *Voices from Slavery: 100 Authentic Slave Narratives* (Toronto: General Publishing Company, Ltd., 2000), 298. The female slave who forgot to put onions in the stew was so traumatized by the torture that she committed suicide. Word has it that her spirit returned to haunt the master and he later committed suicide.

3. Sojourner Truth, *Narrative of Sojourner Truth* (New York: Arno Press and the New York Times, 1968), 26.

4. Nathan Irvin Huggins, *Black Odyssey: The Afro-American Ordeal in Slavery* (New York: Pantheon Books, 1977), 145.

5. James L. Smith, *Autobiography of James L. Smith* (Norwich, Conn.: Press of the Bulletin Company, 1881), 12.

6. Truth, *Narrative of Sojourner Truth*, 85.

7. *Born in Slavery: Slave Narratives from the Federal Writers' Project,* Texas Narratives, vol. 16, part 1, 25; Yetman, *Voices from Slavery*, 18-19.

8. *Born in Slavery: Slave Narratives from the Federal Writers' Project,* Florida Narratives, vol. 3, 67.

9. In fact, adults and children were required to pick 150 pounds of cotton each day. *Born in Slavery: Slave Narratives from the Federal Writers' Project,* Georgia Narratives, vol. 4, part 2, 175. A slaveholder required the ninety-nine-year-old South Carolina ex-slave Mary Raines to work in the cotton fields at the age of twelve. She said, "'long wid de grown ones, [I] pick my 150 pounds of cotton." *Born in Slavery: Slave Narratives from the Federal Writers' Project,* South Carolina Narratives, vol. 14, part 4, 2. The Texas ex-slave John Walton, born in 1849, also said, "Even us kids had to pick 150 pounds of cotton a day, or get a whoppin'." *Born in Slavery: Slave Narratives from the Federal Writers' Project,* Texas Narratives, vol. 16, part 4, 125.

10. William Goodell, *The American Slave Code in Theory and Practice: Its Distinctive Features Shown by Its Statutes, Judicial Decisions, and Illustrative Facts,* (New York: American and Foreign Anti-Slavery Society, 1853), pt. 1, ch. 10, 132-33.

11. *Born in Slavery: Slave Narratives from the Federal Writers' Project,* Florida Narratives, vol. 3, 129.

12. Peter J. Parish, *Slavery: Historians and History* (New York: Harper & Row Publishers, 1989), 40.

13. *Born in Slavery: Slave Narratives from the Federal Writers' Project,* Florida Narratives, vol. 3, 168-69.

14. *Born in Slavery: Slave Narratives from the Federal Writers' Project,* Georgia Narratives, vol. 4, part 1, 24-25.

15. Moses Grandy, *Narrative of the Life of Moses Grandy, Late a Slave in the United States of America* (Boston: O. Johnson Publishing Co., 1844), 18.

16. Yetman, *Voices from Slavery,* 335

CHAPTER FIVE

Public Whippings: A Terrible Part of Living

Most masters and overseers administered public whippings and forced all their slaves to attend; consequently, the slaves were terrified when they saw the suffering and heard the horrible screams of their brutalized brothers and sisters. For example, when the Oklahoma ex-slave Ester Easter observed a runaway slave-boy chained to a whipping post, she was "full of misery" when she saw the lash cutting deep into the boy's skin.[1] An ex-slave from South Carolina, Susan Hamilton, commented on the terror she experienced from the brutality she saw. She said,

> When any slaves was whipped all de other slaves was made to watch. I see women hung from de ceilin' of buildin's and whipped with only sumpin' tied 'round her lower parts of de body . . . dere wasn't breath in de body. I had some terribly bad experiences.[2]

On those plantations where slave hands were not compelled to watch the brutal whippings, they still heard them. Delia Garlic said, "Folks a mile away could hear those awful whippings. Dey was a terrible part of livin'."[3] The Texas ex-slave Lewis Bonner recalled as well hearing the slaves on nearby plantations hollering from their whippings.[4] Another former slave from Texas, Sam Kilgore, similarly said that the slaves on his plantation behaved because they would overhear the slaves on the neighboring plantation "pleadin' when dey's whipped, 'Massa have mercy!' and such."[5] "They were subjected to pain so that it not only seared their own flesh," wrote the historian Nathan Irvin Huggins, "but that their cries would make the skin of others crawl."[6] As we can see, the mere sound of torture instilled in the slaves a paralyzing fear of their masters.

The historian Herbert Aptheker observed that most slaveholders "urged an out and out policy of blood and iron."[7] In those difficult circumstances, the slaves could turn nowhere for protection, as all the power was concentrated in the hands of their oppressors. Masters murdered an incalculable number of slaves. For stealing, a North Carolina slave endured one hundred lashes a day for nine days, but on the ninth day he died.[8] After the owner of the Texas ex-slave Ben Simpson got in trouble in Georgia, he bought two horses and a covered-wagon and made his slaves walk all the way to Texas. In the following excerpt from his narrative, Simpson gives a horrific account of what he saw:

> Massa have a great long whip platted out of rawhide, and when the niggers fall behind or give out, he hit them with that whip. Mother, she give out on the way 'bout the line of Texas. Her feet got raw and bleedin' and her legs swoll plum out of shape. Then massa, he jus' take out he gun and shot her, and whilst she lay dyin' he kicks her two, three times and say, "Damn a nig-ger what can't stand nothin'!" Boss, you know that man, he wouldn't bury mother; jus' leave her layin' where he shot her at.[9]

Travelers from the North observed slave whippings as well. While in North Carolina between 1824 and 1835, Nehemiah Caulkins of Waterford, Connecticut noted, "Scarcely a day passed while I was on the plantation, in which some slaves were not whipped; I do not mean that they were struck a few blows merely, but had a set flogging."[10] Overwhelmed by the torture and suffering she saw in South Carolina, in 1862 the Northern observer Mrs. A. M. French wrote,

> Every face, everything, bears the impress of it. In this dark land, torture has been a science, perfecting for long, long, weary years . . . . We had deter-mined as far as possible, to avoid description of sufferings, for adequately to do it is impossible. Accordingly no instance is given but to illustrate some principle. Still, many instances are pressing upon our mind, as important to the true picture of slavery here. . . . [Slaveholders] have shown out their true character, and now these facts are patent here. We sincerely regret, and blush for shame, that we must speak so of our countrymen.[11]

If the master did not whip his slaves for lagging behind in their labor, he whipped them as a matter of course—as a way of keeping the system intact. Restricted by his imagination only, the slaveholder used all forms of violence to maintain full control. Most slaves were publicly whipped, but others were publicly hanged, burned at the stake, or broken on the wheel, and their heads paraded on poles before their oppressed brothers and sisters. Slaveholders am-putated slaves' fingers, toes, and ears as well.[12] Although the latter forms of torture did not render those slaves unable to work, the sight of that torture cre-ated fear in the hearts of their brothers and sisters.

Treatment Too Awful to Tell

We probably would encounter difficulty finding a pro-slavery writer who would not have downplayed the horrors of American slavery. On the other side, many former slaves were no more inclined to reveal their brutal treatment or to exaggerate the number and severity of their whippings. In some of the federally-funded WPA interviews conducted during the 1930s, former slaves were predisposed to concealing the brutality.[13] Perhaps they were tight-lipped because they feared retribution. After all, the interviews were conducted over seventy years ago in the Jim Crow South. At that time, convinced that many former slaves only privately revealed the horrors of American slavery, the ninety-year-old Texas ex-slave Martin Jackson said,

> Lots of old slaves close the door before they tell the truth about their slavery days. When the door is open, they tell how kind their masters w[ere] and how rosy it all was. You can't blame them for this, because they had a plenty of early discipline, making them cautious about saying anything uncomplimentary about their masters.[14]

Perhaps other elderly ex-slaves were less than forthright about their treatment because they simply did not want to expose the younger interviewers to the unspeakable torment they endured. For example, the Georgia ex-slave Mollie Kinsey said, "Oh! You is blessed to live in this day and don't know the tortures the slaves went through."[15] Susan McIntosh, another former slave from Georgia, similarly told her interviewer, "There ain't no need to think of them times now."[16] The comments of the ninety-five-year-old Virginia ex-slave Elizabeth Sparks are indicative of the sentiments of other interviewed ex-slaves. She stated, "Well I kin tell yer, but I ain't. S'all past now, so I say let 'er rest —'s too awful to tell anyway." When her interviewer questioned her about the severity of the torture, Sparks replied, "Yer're too young to know all that talk anyway. Well I'll tell yer some to put in yer book, but I ain'ta goin' to tell yer the worse."[17]

Notes

1. Norman Y. Yetman, ed., *Voices from Slavery: 100 Authentic Slave Narratives* (Toronto: General Publishing Company, Ltd., 2000), 108.

2. George P. Rawick, ed., *The American Slave: A Composite Autobiography*, 41 vols. (Westport, Conn.: Greenwood Publishing Co., 1972), South Carolina, part 2, 27.

3. Yetman, *Voices from Slavery*, 133.

4. *Born in Slavery: Slave Narratives from the Federal Writers' Project, 1936-1938* (Wash., D.C.: Library of Congress, 2001), Oklahoma Narratives, vol. 13, 17. <http://memory.loc.gov/ammem/snhtml> (15 April 2006).

5. Yetman, *Voices from Slavery*, 196.

6. Nathan Irvin Huggins, *Black Odyssey: The Afro-American Ordeal in Slavery* (New York: Pantheon Books, 1977), 122.

7. Herbert Aptheker, *American Negro Slave Revolts* (New York: International Publishers, 1983), 59.

8. Rawick, *The American Slave*, North Carolina, part 1, 30.

9. *Born in Slavery: Slave Narratives from the Federal Writers' Project*, Texas Narratives, vol. 16, part 4, 27.

10. Rev. Theodore D. Weld et al, ed., *Slavery as It Is: Testimony of a Thousand Witnesses* (New York: American Anti-Slavery Society, 1839), 13.

11. Mrs. A. M. French, *Slavery in South Carolina and the Ex-slaves; or, The Port Royal Mission* (New York: Winchell M. French, 1862; reprinted New York: Negro Universities Press, 1969), 49-51.

12. Weld, *Slavery as It Is*, 78-79.

13. John C. Perry estimates that "an overwhelming majority" of those ex-slaves reported that their owners were "good people." John C. Perry, *Myths & Realities of American Slavery* (Shippensburg, Pa.: Burd Street Press, 2002), 135. However, Peter Kolchin advises, "The relative freedom afforded many slave children is one reason that the Federal Writers' Project interviews must be used with extreme caution in reconstructing the lives of adults; two-thirds of those interviewed were born after 1850 and were thus ten years old or younger at the outbreak of the Civil War." Peter Kolchin, *American Slavery 1619-1877* (New York: Hill and Wang, 1993), 141. Many were born slaves but were too young to experience the evils of slavery.

14. Yetman, *Voices from Slavery*, 174-75.

15. Andrew Waters, ed., *On Jordan's Stormy Banks* (Winston-Salem: John F. Blair, Publisher, 2000), 21-22.

16. Waters, *On Jordan's Stormy Banks*, 167.

17. *Born in Slavery: Slave Narratives from the Federal Writers' Project*, Virginia Narratives, vol. 17, 50.

CHAPTER SIX

White Man's Law: Black Man's Grief

"There is a law above all statutes written on the heart, and by that law, un-changeable and eternal, no man can be or hold a slave."

—FREDERICK DOUGLASS,
My Bondage and My Freedom,
1855

While the torture of individual slaves on the plantation was the first way of controlling the slave population, slaveholder-created legal constraints were the second way. Laws enacted throughout the South during the late eighteenth and early nineteenth centuries by the slaveholding class—commonly referred to as slave codes—defined the legal relationship between the master and his slave. It is important for us to understand that the slave was not a person in the eyes of the law; he was chattel—his master's personal property. Since he was not considered a person, the slave codes neither afforded him protection, nor were intended to give him any.

In fact, the slaveholding class enacted laws for its own protection. By 1860, slaveowners constituted three-quarters of deep-South legislators and two-thirds of upper-South legislators.[1] As an unparalleled political force, they not only made the law but they tried the "offenders" and administered the penalties. By virtue of their acquired political and economic power, they shaped the legal system to their interests and in the process created a Southern regional view compatible with their regime. The judicial system became the instrument by which the slaveholding class tried to impose its viewpoint upon the wider society—not excluding the slaves themselves. The goal was to make slavery so acceptable that no Southerner would question it. Thus, those who questioned or disturbed the regime would become enemies of Southern white society itself.[2]

Southern states passed laws prohibiting the circulation of abolitionist literature and outlawing discussion of anti-slavery doctrines.[3] The slaveholding class then used those laws to stifle anti-slavery opinion and discourage slave resistance.

In the ante-bellum South, the white man's law was the black man's grief. Slave codes empowered the slaveholder and silenced his slave, rendering the latter powerless. The laws gave the master the license—indeed made it his duty—to torture his slaves toward an end of securing total and unconditional submission, while they prohibited the slaves from complaining about the inhumane treatment.[4]

In examining slave codes throughout the ante-bellum South, we find three significant common threads. The first is that they prevented slaves and free persons of color from testifying against any white person. The former slave and abolitionist Frederick Douglass wrote, "Laws for the protection of the lives of the slaves are . . . utterly incapable of being enforced, where the very parties who are nominally protected, are not permitted to give evidence, in courts of law, against the only class of persons from whom abuse, outrage and murder might be reasonably apprehended."[5] Slave codes in the states of North Carolina, Virginia, Missouri, Louisiana, Mississippi, Alabama, Maryland, Tennessee, and even the free state of Ohio, barred blacks—slaves and free— from testifying against whites.[6] One example of such a law is the following Commonwealth of Virginia slave code:

> Any negro or mulatto, bond or free, shall be a good witness in pleas of the Commonwealth, for or against negroes or mulattoes, bond or free, or in civil pleas where free negroes or mulattoes shall alone be parties, *and in no other cases whatever.*[7]

Though a slave code in South Carolina and a Louisiana slave code of 1816 also prevented blacks from testifying against whites, modifications of the law in those states (enacted purportedly to give slaves at least some protection against malicious acts committed by a master and resulting in a slave's loss of life, limb or member) still gave protection to cruel masters and overseers. The slave codes in those states provided that where no white person saw a slaveholder take his slave's life, limb or member or where no white person was willing to testify against the owner, the owner or other person having charge of that slave was deemed guilty and punished, unless the owner or other person could "make the contrary appear by good and sufficient evidence" or, "by his own oath, clear and exculpate himself." The court administering the oath exercised its authority to acquit the alleged offender when clear proof of the offense was not offered by at least two witnesses.[8] Otherwise stated, if, for example, a master maliciously murdered his slave, he could clear himself of the charge by testifying on his own behalf that he did not do so maliciously, and he could avoid punishment if no more than one white witness came forward and testified to the contrary. Since the slave codes prohibited slaves from testifying against whites and therefore precluded them from establishing the required evidentiary proof that a master maliciously murdered his slave, in most instances that master was beyond the reach of the law.

The second common thread among slave codes enacted in most Southern states was a provision permitting a master to murder his slave and to avoid punishment if the slave resisted his command. In 1798 and 1799 the states of North Carolina and Tennessee passed laws permitting the murder of "any slave in the act of resistance to his lawful owner or master, or any slave dying under moderate correction."[9] Under North Carolina law, an owner who maliciously killed his slave could suffer the same punishment as if he had killed a free man, but only on the condition that a white person saw the act and was willing to testify against him.

The Georgia Constitution of 1798 sanctioned the murder of any slave "in case of insurrection of said slave" or "if such death should happen by accident in giving such slave moderate correction."[10] Thus, under Georgia law, we also find that if a master were to murder a rebellious slave or were to accidentally whip a slave to death through "moderate correction," he would incur no penalty. One example of the law's ineffectiveness in protecting slaves' lives is provided by the Georgia ex-slave Shade Richards. He told us that his owner's son, "Mr. Jimmy," often whipped his slaves to death, but he was never prosecuted. In fact, Richards said that his uncle was murdered in that manner by his master's son.[11]

Similar to North Carolina law, under Georgia law, a slaveholder who maliciously dismembered a slave, or maliciously deprived a slave of life, suffered the same punishment as would have been inflicted had he committed the same offense upon a free white person if a white witness saw the act and testified successfully against him.[12] Slave murder laws promulgated in the states of Alabama in 1819, Missouri in 1820, and Texas in 1845 were patterned on Georgia's model.[13]

A South Carolina Act of 1740 permitted any person in a sudden heat of passion or by "undue correction" to "kill his own slave, or the slave of any other person," provided he forfeited a sum of £350. As amended in 1821, the Act increased the penalty for killing a slave in a sudden heat or by undue correction to $500 or imprisonment for six months.[14]

We might ask, "What was undue correction?" If it was correction that was not warranted or excessive correction, who determined whether or not the correction was unwarranted or excessive? Since we know that the slaves had no say in the matter, we may postulate that if a slaveholder in South Carolina after the year 1821 were to kill his slave in a sudden heat of passion, or were to unduly correct him by whipping or beating him to death, in the absence of a white witness, that slaveholder probably would not have been fined or imprisoned. In the exceptional circumstance where another white person would have seen the act and been willing to testify against him, the penalty permitting the master to murder his slave would have been only $500 or imprisonment for six months.

Laws against the mistreatment of slaves were not only ineffective in deterring murderous treatment; they were not rigorously enforced. Frederick Douglass noted that while he heard of numerous murders committed by slaveowners in east coastal Maryland, he "never knew a solitary instance in which a slaveholder was either hung or imprisoned for having murdered a slave."[15] In the final analysis, enslaved black people in the ante-bellum South could not look to the laws for protection from the caprice and cruelty of their owners.

Insofar as slave codes throughout the ante-bellum South permitted a master to murder his slave and avoid punishment, the third common thread among these codes was that they made the slave entirely subject to his owner's will. They allowed a master to do just about anything that he wanted to do with his slave, and that slave was compelled to obey his command. Given that, we might imagine all of the uses to which human chattel were put by the slaveholder. With the exception of a South Carolina slave code, which limited to fifteen the number of daily labor hours a slaveholder was allowed to take from his slave, slave codes in most of the Southern states permitted a master to work his slave as long as he wanted to work him.[16] The historian John Hope Franklin found that on the Louisiana sugar-cane plantations it was not uncommon for the slave drivers to work the slaves up to twenty hours each day during the harvest season.[17]

The slave codes permitted the master to breed his chattel as well—to arbitrarily assign a slave-woman a sex mate and force her to bear slave-children. They allowed the master (and non-slaveholding whites acting on his directive) to rape his slave-women and sell the mulatto offspring, if any, for profit. Laws governing the master-slave relationship permitted the slaveholder to sell his slaves to pay debts, to sell his bondswomen into prostitution, and even to dispose of his ill slaves by selling them to medical science for research and experimentation. On October 12, 1838, the following advertisement by Dr. T. Stillman on behalf of the "Medical Infirmary" appeared in the *Charleston Mercury*, a South Carolina newspaper of the time:

TO PLANTERS AND OTHERS.—Wanted, *fifty negroes*. Any person, having sick negroes, considered incurable by their respective physicians, and wishing to dispose of them, Dr. S. will *pay cash* for negroes affected with scrofula, or king's evil, confirmed hypochondriasm, apoplexy, diseases of the liver, kidneys, spleen, stomach and intestines, bladder and its appendages, diarrhœa, dysentery, &c. *The highest cash price* will be paid, on application as above," (viz., "Medical Infirmary, No. 110 Church Street, Charleston.")[18]

As a practical matter, if a slave tried to resist any of the many uses to which his owner may have put him, statutes prohibiting the slave's murder afforded him no protection; generally, a slave who simply disobeyed his master's command could be killed by that master, and the master would serve no prison time. The Florida ex-slave Taylor Gilbert understood the consequences of the slave codes for the slave caught off his plantation without a pass. He recalled that often the slaveholders' sons "would go 'nigger hunting' and nothing—not even murder—was too horrible for them to do to slaves caught without passes." Gilbert said that they would justify the murder of a bondsman by claiming that the slave disobeyed their command—by simply saying, "The 'nigger' tried to run away when told to stop."[19]

In virtually all cases of masters who murdered their slaves, the masters were not prosecuted criminally. The traveler Charles William Janson observed that when the "bloody deed" was committed, it was in fact seldom looked into.[20] On that rare occasion where a criminal proceeding was commenced against a slaveholder accused of killing his slave, the homicide of that slave typically would end in an acquittal; in his own defense, the master would testify that his slave had legally provoked him.[21] Any resistance offered by a slave sufficed as legal provocation, making the killing of that slave lawful. Consequently, even when a court investigated a master's murder of his slave, the slaveholder could assume its sympathy and reap the benefit of its presumption that no rational slaveowner would willfully and maliciously kill his valuable human property.[22] Because Ben Simpson saw his master kill his slave-mother and go unpunished, cognizant of the fact that slaveholders were hardly ever held accountable for murdering their slaves, he concluded, "You know, then there wasn't no law 'gainst killin' nigger slaves."[23]

The slaveholding class used its laws to violently suppress slave revolts. During the last three decades of the ante-bellum era, eleven states passed laws imposing the death penalty on slaves who participated in insurrections. For example, a Georgia law of 1843 and a Virginia law of 1848 made insurrection or an attempt to incite it—whether directly or indirectly—punishable by death. In thirteen states, it became a capital crime for free men to incite a slave to insurrection.

Severe penalties were levied against anyone who helped a slave to run away or who gave him asylum after he escaped.[24] But what about the runaway slave? The Commonwealth of Virginia passed the following legislation, recognizing that the repression of runaway slaves may be carried to the point of murder:

> . . . it would be lawful for any person or persons whatsoever to kill and destroy such [runaway] slaves by such ways and means as he, she or they should think fit, without accusation or impeachment for any crime of the same . . . .[25]

Slaves who committed the same crimes as white persons suffered from harsher penalties. For example, the laws of Maryland sentenced any slave convicted of petty larceny, murder, or willfully burning dwelling houses "to have the right hand cut off; to be hanged in the usual manner, the head severed from the body, the body divided into four quarters, and the head and quarters set up in the most public places of the county, where such act was committed."[26] Since the law sanctioned the most savage acts of violence imaginable, some slaveholders did not hesitate to commit them. Harriet Martineau, a traveler journeying through the Old South, wrote, "Burning alive, cutting the heart out and sticking it on the point of a knife . . . the result of the deepest hatred of which the human heart is capable, are heard of . . . here."[27] Whether there were two or twenty of those legally-sanctioned public acts of violence each year, surely they instilled deep-seated fear in the slaves and testified to the existence of a deep inhumanity and pathology which alone can explain them.

Southern state legislatures were not the only bodies that enacted repressive slave laws. On September 18, 1850, Congress amended the Fugitive Slave Act to make both state and federal governments responsible for capturing runaway slaves and returning them to their owners. Federal law subjected those aiding or harboring runaways or interfering with their capture to fines or imprisonment.[28] As the historian Mary Frances Berry observed, "The federal government worked vigorously to enforce the new act and to suppress attempted violations."[29]

Notes

1. Peter Kolchin, *American Slavery 1619-1877* (New York: Hill and Wang, 1993), 184.

2. Herbert Aptheker, *American Negro Slave Revolts* (New York: International Publishers, 1983), 56.

3. Mary Frances Berry, *Black Resistance White Law: A History of Constitutional Racism in America* (New York: Allen Lane The Penguin Press, 1994), 54.

4. Thomas D. Morris, *Southern Slavery and the Law 1619-1860* (Chapel Hill: University of North Carolina Press, 1996), 161.

5. Frederick Douglass, *My Bondage and My Freedom* (Chicago: Johnson Publishing Co., 1970), p. 99.

6. (Virginia, 1 Revised Code, 422.) (Missouri Laws, 600.) (Mississippi, Revised Code, 372.) (Kentucky, 2 Littell and Swigert's Digest, 1150.) (Alabama, Toulmin's Dig., 627.) (Maryland Laws, Act of 1717, Chap. 13, Sects. 2, 3; and Act of 1751, Chap. 14, Sect. 4.) (North Carolina and Tennessee, Act of 1777, Chap. 2, Sect. 42.) (Ohio, Act of January 25, 1807). William Goodell, *The American Slave Code in Theory and Practice: Its Distinctive Features Shown by Its Statutes, Judicial Decisions, and Illustrative Facts* (New York: American and Foreign Anti-Slavery Society, 1853), part 2, ch. 3, 300-301.

7. (Virginia, 1 Revised Code, 422.) Goodell, *The American Slave Code*, part 2, ch. 3, 300. (emphasis mine)

8. Goodell, *The American Slave Code*, part 2, ch. 3, 301.

9. In North Carolina, an Act of 1798 provided:

If any person hereafter be guilty of maliciously killing a slave, such offender shall, on the first conviction thereof, be adjudged guilty of murder, and shall suffer the same punishment as if he had killed a free man: Provided always, this act shall not extend to any person killing a slave outlawed by virtue of any Act of Assembly of this State, *or* to any slave in the act of *resistance* to his lawful owner or master, *or* to any slave dying under moderate correction.

The state of Tennessee, by an Act of October 23, 1799, passed a law similar to that of North Carolina. Goodell, *The American Slave Code,* part 1, ch. 14, 180-82.

10. Francis Newton Thorpe, *The Federal and State Constitutions,* 7 vols. (Wash., D.C.: U.S. Government Printing Office, 1909) vol. 2, 801; Goodell, *The American Slave Code,* part 1, ch. 14, 183.

11. *Born in Slavery: Slave Narratives from the Federal Writers' Project,* Georgia Narratives, vol. 4, part 3, 202.

12. *Born in Slavery: Slave Narratives from the Federal Writers' Project,* Georgia Narratives, vol. 4, part 3, 202.

13. Morris, *Southern Slavery and the Law,* 172.

14. Goodell, *The American Slave Code,* part 1, ch. 14, 179.

15. Douglass, *My Bondage and My Freedom,* 99.

16. A Georgia law, enacted in 1852, did prohibit "requiring greater labor from such slave or slaves, than he, she or they are able to perform"; however, it did not impose an hourly slave-labor limit. Morris, *Southern Slavery and the Law,* 196.

17. John Hope Franklin and Alfred A. Moss Jr., *From Slavery to Freedom,* 6th ed. (New York: Alfred A. Knopf, Inc., 1988), 117.

18. Goodell, *The American Slave Code,* part 1, ch. 5, 87.

19. *Born in Slavery: Slave Narratives from the Federal Writers' Project,* Florida Narratives, vol. 3, 223-24.

20. Charles William Janson, *Stranger in America 1793-1806* (New York: The Press of Pioneers, Inc., 1935), 364.

21. Morris, *Southern Slavery and the Law,* 181.

22. Nathan Irvin Huggins, *Black Odyssey: The Afro-American Ordeal in Slavery* (New York: Pantheon Books, 1977), 148.

23. *Born in Slavery: Slave Narratives from the Federal Writers' Project,* Texas Narratives, vol. 16, part 4, 27.

24. Robert W. Fogel and Stanley L. Engerman, *Time on the Cross* (Boston: Little, Brown & Co., 1974), 37.

25. Edmund S. Morgan, *American Slavery, American Freedom* (New York: W. W. Norton & Co., Inc., 1975), 312.

26. Goodell, *The American Slave Code,* part 2, ch. 5, 316.

27. Harriet Martineau, *Society in America,* vol. 2 (London: Saunders and Otley, 1837), 329.

28. Section 7 of the Fugitive Slave Act of 1850 provided:

That any person who shall knowingly and willingly obstruct, hinder or prevent such claimant, his agent or attorney, or any person or persons lawfully assisting him, her or them, from arresting such a fugitive from service or labor, either with or without process as aforesaid, or shall rescue or attempt to rescue, such fugitive from service or labor, from the custody of such claimant, his or her agent or attorney, or other person or persons lawfully assisting as aforesaid, when so arrested, pursuant to the authority herein given and declared; or shall aid, abet or assist such person so owing service or labor as aforesaid, directly or indirectly, to escape from such claimant, his agent or attorney, or other person or persons legally authorized as aforesaid; or shall harbor or conceal such fugitive, so as to prevent the discovery and arrest of such person, after notice or knowledge of the fact that such person was a fugitive from service or labor as aforesaid, shall, for either of said offences, be subject to a fine not exceeding one thousand dollars, and imprisonment not exceeding six months, by indictment and conviction before the District Court of the United States for the district in which such offence may have been committed, or before the proper court of criminal jurisdiction, if committed within any one of the organized Territories of the United States; and shall moreover forfeit and pay, by way of civil damages to the party injured by such illegal conduct, the sum of one thousand dollars for each fugitive so lost as aforesaid, to be recovered by action in debt, in any of the district or Territorial Courts aforesaid, within whose jurisdiction the said offence may have been committed.

29. Berry, *Black Resistance White Law*, 56.

CHAPTER SEVEN

The Omnipresent Slave Patrols

The last major form of physical repression was the omnipresent slave patrol system. Because they were alarmed by the Nat Turner Insurrection of 1831, slaveholders in the South reinforced fear in black people by organizing night slave patrols. We know that about three-quarters of Southern white families did not own slaves, but it was non-slaveholding whites who were given responsibility for enforcing laws restricting the movement of slaves.[1] The Alabama courts, for example, compelled every non-slaveholder under the age of forty-five to perform patrol duty.[2] Those informal civilian armies constituted what the historian Nathan Irvin Huggins called "the arm of community power against slaves."[3] Unless they first obtained written permission from their owners, the slaves were prohibited by slave codes throughout the ante-bellum South from leaving their plantations and moving about unattended at night.[4] Basically run by poor white men, the patrols played the major role in limiting slave movement. The historian Leslie Howard Owens noted, "Sometimes financed by a small tax on slaves above the age of twelve, and sometimes voluntary, it was an obvious way for whites to guard against slave resistance while making sure the slaves remained careful of their moves."[5]

A system of patrol existed in every slaveholding state. Courts were empowered to appoint one or more patrols for terms not exceeding three months to survey all slave quarters and arrest those slaves caught off their masters' plantations without passes. Generally, members of a patrol worked in rotations of two-to-three-week periods to spread the responsibility for policing, and some counties in the South imposed small fines upon individuals who neglected to perform their patrol duties. By 1845, Georgia law required every person appointed to slave patrol duty who evaded it to pay a five dollar fine.[6]

Justices of the peace in each district of the state of Georgia were authorized to determine eligibility for and appointment to patrol duty. The laws of that state required every slave patrol member to carry a pistol while on duty.

They also gave the patroller authority to capture fugitive slaves, search slaves for weapons, and whip them—typically by administering twenty lashes.[7]

Even in those regions in the South where patrol methods were inefficient, the patrol system nonetheless left with the slave community the perception of pervasive repression. To neutralize the enormous military advantage concentrated in the hands of the slaveholding class, the slaves required power in numbers; however, in the last three decades of the ante-bellum period, blacks outnumbered whites in only two slaveholding states.[8] Although some trusted slaves had arms, most did not. As the political economist Manning Marable wrote,

> Some Afro-Americans would be permitted to bear arms within the coercive apparatuses of the state, so long as [they] were fighting to protect the capitalist political economy and civil society of white racism. Within the ideological apparatuses and civil society, a strict policy of black disarmament was upheld.[9]

Blacks outnumbered whites in South Carolina.[10] The law in that state forbade slaves possessing legal permits to be armed to carry weapons in public between Saturday night and Monday morning. No more than one slave on any single plantation was permitted to carry a gun.[11] By comparison, in the white population, noted Eugene Genovese, "Sharp-shooting and extraordinary feats with arms became elementary marks of manhood. [Whites] constituted one great militia—fully and even extravagantly armed . . . and capable of all the savagery that racism can instill."[12]

If the slave were fortunate enough to endure the torment he suffered on the plantation and survive under the ante-bellum South's repressive slave codes, the slave patrols would remain for him a formidable barrier to freedom, rendering virtually all avenues of escape unsafe. Most slaves feared the slave patrols.[13] A former slave from Georgia, Julie Brown, told us that the slave "was 'fraid to go any place" because of the patrols.[14] Henry Bibb wrote, "Running away . . . the night being dark . . . among the slaveholders and the slave hunters . . . was like a person entering the wilderness among wolves and vipers, blindfolded."[15] The Georgia ex-slave Rachel Adams recalled, "Slaves never went nowhere without them patterollers beatin' 'em up if they didn't have no pass."[16] Sam T. Stewart, a former slave from North Carolina, said that when patrollers caught slaves off the plantation where no whipping posts were available, they tied them across fences to whip them.[17] Celestia Avery remembered being told by a slave-woman about the occasion her Uncle William was caught off the Heard plantation without a pass and "whipped almost to death by the 'parder rollers.'"[18] Some slaves would not have told their owners about the whippings for fear of being tortured again.

The Oklahoma ex-slave Anthony Dawson and other former slaves would sing a song, revealing all too well their awareness of the armed slave patrols.

Dawson wondered whether or not Southern whites made up the following song to keep the slaves in line:[19]

> Run Nigger, run, de Patteroll get you!
> Run Nigger, run, de Patteroll come!
> Watch Nigger, watch, de Patteroll trick you!
> Watch Nigger, watch, he got a big gun![20]

Slaves were especially antagonistic toward slave patrols and slave hunters because many overstepped their bounds. Some slave patrollers disrupted slave social gatherings and religious meetings.[21] Others raped slave-women.[22] Slave hunters subjected captured runaways to cruel and unusual treatment. The ex-slave Jacob Stroyer never forgot a South Carolina slave hunter named Mr. Black who was the most barbarous one he knew. Stroyer wrote,

> [A runaway] was with another, who was thought well of by his master. The second of whom . . . killed several dogs and gave Messrs. Black and Motley a hard fight. After the Negro had been captured they killed him, cut him up and gave his remains to the dogs.[23]

During the Civil War, local governments in the South tightened restrictions on the movement all black people. On February 7, 1862, for instance, the city of Augusta, Georgia passed the following ordinance, limiting the movement of slaves and free persons of color:

> Any slave or free person of color found riding or driving about the city, not having a written pass from his or her owner, hirer, or guardian, expressing the date of such pass, the name of the negro to whom it is given, the place or places to which he is going, how long he or she is to be absent, and in the case of a slave, that such a slave is in the services of the person before the re-corder's court by which he or she shall be tried, and on conviction shall be punished by whipping not to exceed 39 lashes.[24]

Increased fines were imposed as well on slaveowners who allowed their property to move about unattended. As the historian Mary Frances Berry noted, "Patrol duty was made a more regular function with increased fines for the failure to perform such duty, and laws requiring white male supervision of slaves on plantations were stringently enforced."[25]

Toward an Accurate Account of American Slavery

In Part One, we examined historiography on the brutality of American slavery. By and large, the scholarship shows a preoccupation with rationalizing and de-emphasizing the slaveowner's horrible acts. Instead of exposing his true disposition, many American historians prefer to defend his humanity by depicting him in a favorable light. In fact, they search for any redeeming qualities in the slaveholder. As a consequence, the true nature and character of the American slavery regime is concealed. W. L. Post told us, "Them was bad times, them was bad times. I know folks think the books tell the truth but they sure don't. Us poor niggers had to take it all."[26] Perhaps Martin Jackson said it best: "I can tell you the life of the average slave was not rosy. They were dealt out plenty of cruel suffering."[27] An accurate portrayal of the American slavery regime should reveal the fiendish methods of individual torture used by the slaveholding class and show how that torture, the repressive slave codes, and the vicious system of slave patrols created fear in the slave community and prevented widespread slave revolts.

During the ante-bellum period, another violent act of repression—rarely examined today in that context—was the rape of the black bondswoman. At a time during which feminist literature should have clarified our understanding of rape, studies on master-on-slave rape are wanting in probing analysis. Why did slaveholders rape their black female captives? In Part Two, we will scrutinize influential American historians' treatment of the subject of master-on-slave rape and examine that specific mode of repression.

Notes

1. John C. Perry, *Myths & Realities of American Slavery* (Shippensburg, Pa.: Burd Street Press, 2002), 97. However, as the historian Peter J. Parish points out, "If attention is confined to the states that eventually became a part of the Confederacy, 31 % of white families owned slaves in 1860. In South Carolina and Mississippi, almost half the white families owned slaves; in four more states of the Deep South, one-third or more of the white families owned slaves." Parish, *Slavery: History and Historians* (New York: Harper & Row Publishers, 1989), 28.

2. Henry Bibb, *Narrative of the Life and Adventures of Henry Bibb, an American Slave* (New York: H. Bibb, 1849), 76.

3. Nathan Irvin Huggins, *Black Odyssey: The Afro-American Ordeal in Slavery* (New York: Pantheon Books, 1977), 123.

4. Lester B. Shippee, ed., *Bishop Whipple's Southern Diary 1843-44* (Minneapolis: University of Minnesota Press, 1937), 182.

5. Leslie Howard Owens, *This Species of Property* (New York: Oxford University Press, Inc., 1976), 73.

6. *Born in Slavery: Slave Narratives from the Federal Writers' Project, 1936-1938*, (Wash., D.C.: Library of Congress, 2001) Georgia Narratives, vol. 4, part 4, 322. <memory.loc.gov/ammem/snhtml/snhome> (4 June 2007).

7. *Born in Slavery: Slave Narratives from the Federal Writers' Project*, Georgia Narratives, vol. 4, part 4, 322.

8. Blacks outnumbered whites in South Carolina and Mississippi. *Statistics of the Population of the United States, Embracing the Tables of Race, Nationality, Sex, Selected Ages and Occupations . . . Compiled from the Original Returns of the Ninth Census (June 1, 1870)* (Wash., D.C.: U.S. Government Printing Office, 1872), 4-7.

9. Manning Marable, "The Military, Black People and the Racist State: A History of Coercion," *Black Scholar* 12, no. 1 (January/February 1981): 9.

10. In 1850, there were 274,563 whites, 384,984 slaves, and 8,960 free blacks in South Carolina. A decade later, there were 291,300 whites, 402,406 slaves, and 9,914 free blacks in that state. *Statistics of the Population of the United States*, 4-7.

11. Marable, "The Military, Black People and the Racist State," 9; John Hope Franklin, *From Slavery to Freedom* (New York: Vintage Books, 1969), 79, 85.

12. Eugene D. Genovese, *From Rebellion to Revolution* (New York: Vintage Books, 1979), 16.

13. Norman Y. Yetman, ed., *Voices from Slavery: 100 Authentic Slave Narratives* (Toronto: General Publishing Company, Ltd., 2000), 299.

14. Yetman, *Voices from Slavery*, 47.

15. Bibb, *Narrative of the Life and Adventures of Henry Bibb*, 98.

16. Andrew Waters, ed., *On Jordan's Stormy Banks* (Winston-Salem: John F. Blair, Publisher, 2000), 120.

17. *Born in Slavery: Slave Narratives from the Federal Writers' Project*, North Carolina Narratives, vol. 11, part 2, 320.

18. George P. Rawick, ed., *The American Slave: A Composite Autobiography*, 41 vols. (Westport, Conn.: Greenwood Publishing Co., 1972), Georgia, part 1, 24.

19. Yetman, *Voices from Slavery*, 93.

20. Yetman, *Voices from Slavery*, 93; Rawick, *The American Slave*, Georgia, part 1, 143; Waters, *On Jordan's Stormy Banks*, 34.

21. Yetman, *Voices from Slavery*, 37.

22. Owens, *This Species of Property*, 74.

23. Jacob Stroyer, *My Life in the South* (Salem: Newcomb & Gauss, 1898), 72.

24. *Born in Slavery: Slave Narratives from the Federal Writers' Project*, Georgia Narratives, vol. 4, part 4, 323.

25. Mary Frances Berry, *Black Resistance White Law: A History of Constitutional Racism in America* (New York: Allen Lane The Penguin Press, 1994), 66.

26. Yetman, *Voices from Slavery*, 38.

27. Yetman, *Voices from Slavery*, 174-75.

PART TWO

Master-on-Slave Rape

CHAPTER EIGHT

A Reluctance to Call It Rape

A revered historian of American slavery once asked, "Do we need to be told again that white men took sexual advantage of black women during American slavery?" The answer is not exactly. Depending upon how we interpret the phrase "took sexual advantage of," it could mean anything from a euphemism for rape to a misleading mischaracterization of it. In teaching us about the past, the objective historian searches out the facts, and in conveying those facts, he places candor and clarity above concealment. To that end, we should be told not only that white men customarily raped black women during American slavery, but we should also be told why they did it. Credible explanations for master-on-slave rape are lacking in most history books about slavery primarily because few American slavery historians acknowledge that the rape of black bondswomen was a widespread occurrence, with a calculated purpose behind it.

Any discussion of master-on-slave rape should begin with a working definition of "rape." "Rape" is defined as "unlawful sexual activity" and usually sexual intercourse carried out forcibly or under the threat of injury against the will, usually of a female, or with a person who is beneath a certain age or incapable of valid consent.[1] The feminist Susan Brownmiller broadly defines rape as "nothing more or less than a conscious process of intimidation by which all men keep all women in fear."[2]

Most historians of American slavery agree that in the ante-bellum South the states prosecuted white women's rapes only. As the historian Thomas D. Morris pointed out, the law did not extend the same protection to black women as it did to white women.[3] Her master's personal property, the bondswoman was not a person in the eyes of the law. Thus, the law did not recognize her rape as an offense—unless her owner regarded it as a trespass on his property and brought that charge.[4] Although ante-bellum-era rape laws that denied protection to black women would not be considered equitable or just today, the majority of white Southerners of that period would not have questioned them.

There is also general agreement among historians that during the ante-bellum period not all sexual encounters between white men and bondswomen constituted rape. Consensual sex occurred across racial lines. Relationships based upon genuine mutual desire did develop between some slaveholders and their bondswomen. In 1862, Mrs. A. M. French wrote about Colonel Richard M. Johnson, a South Carolina slaveowner who

> . . . was *so very* singular as to treat the mother of his Colored daughters as though she were his wife; to give her charge of his household; a seat by his side at his table, addressing her as "Mrs. Johnson"—to do all of this, instead of selling her in the market, as some other great statesmen have sold the mothers of their Colored children. When "Mrs. Johnson" became religious and wished to unite with the Church, the good minister felt it his duty to tell her that there was an obstacle in the way—the scandal of her living as she did with Colonel Johnson. She immediately communicated the fact to the Colonel. "You know my dear," said he, "I have always been ready to marry you, whenever it could be done. I am ready now and will call on your minister about it." He did so, and requested the minister to marry them, after explaining the facts of the case. The good minister was now in a worse dilemma than before! What! Marry Colonel Johnson to a *Colored* woman! What could he say! He could only say that the law would not permit such a marriage.[5]

But relationships such as Colonel Johnson's were hardly the norm. Typically, the bondswoman engaged in sexual intercourse with her master, his son, the overseer, the slave trader, or other white men, under the threat of injury and against her will.[6] If rape is sexual intercourse carried out forcibly or under the threat of injury against the will of a woman, why is it that so many historians are reluctant to use the word rape in describing the sexual encounters between slaveholders and their bondswomen? Some of their characterizations of the violent sexual act suggest that the slaveholder typically seduced the bondswoman; he enticed her to sexual intercourse by means other than force. They mask the slaveholder's brutal takeover of the bondswoman's body by using various obfuscatory words and phrases such as philandering, finding pleasure, prostitution, procuring sexual favors, seduction, sexual experimentation, miscegenation, and making love.

Indeed, the language that some American historians (primarily male) employ to conceal nonconsensual sexual intercourse between master and slave-woman suggests that during the ante-bellum period white-on-black rape did not occur routinely. For example, Kenneth Stampp wrote that white men "had sexual relations," "engaged in sexual experimentation," "demanded favors," "succumbed to temptations surrounding them," and "committed miscegenation."[7] The historian and sociologist E. Franklin Frazier, slightly more direct in broaching the subject of master-on-slave rape, found that the character of sexual association between white men and black women ranged from rape to voluntary surrender because he saw in some bonds a mutual attraction and a material advantage to be gained for the bondswoman.[8] Leslie Howard Owens noted that slaveholders "mixed their blood" in the race, "gave expression to their human desires," and "consorted with" bondswomen.[9]

The economic historians Robert W. Fogel and Stanley L. Engerman insisted that white men merely "took on mistresses . . . seduced girls of tender ages, and patronized prostitutes."[10] John Perry characterized the sexual encounters between slaveowners and their bondswomen as "philandering."[11] Is their reluctance to call it rape just coincidental? No it is not. Scholars such as Fogel and Engerman, Perry, and others make no mention of rape or physical coercion in describing what was more often than not nonconsensual sex because they harbor a racist assumption that white men—particularly those who exert economic power—have an undeniable right of access to black women's bodies.[12]

Also reluctant to use the word "rape" in describing nonconsensual sexual intercourse between slaveowner and bondswoman, Eugene Genovese claimed that slaveholders "were tempted into intimacies," "acted out childish fantasies," "sought casual pleasures," "slept with" black women, took advantage of "institutionally structured concubinage," and "quasi-raped" black women.[13] The term "quasi-raped" is bizarre. What does Genovese mean? "Quasi" is defined as having some resemblance to. Is he also suggesting that slaveholders did not rape their slave-women? His claim that sexual encounters between masters and bondswomen typically fell between seduction and rape is of no more help to us. Sexual intercourse does not typically fall between seduction and rape; it occurs and is then either consensual or nonconsensual.

John Blassingame noted that white overseers and slaveholders obtained sexual favors of black women.[14] In a decidedly oxymoronic characterization of the sexual encounters, he also wrote, "Generally speaking, the women were literally forced to offer themselves 'willingly'. . . ."[15]

Role Reversal: Slaveholder as Sufferer of Psychic Agony

Some American male historians have placed master-on-slave rape within the context of emotional involvement and human desire. Kenneth Stampp, for example, argued that sexual encounters between masters and their bondswomen were "very human indeed."[16] Forgiving of the slaveholder and defensive of his humanity, Stampp's mischaracterization of the violent sexual encounters underscores the emotional ties that certain masters developed with their slave-women—albeit after the violent acts.[17] This is mischaracterization at the bondswoman's expense; he and others humanize the master by focusing on either his emotional involvement or his psychic agony and troubled conscience, while they dehumanize the bondswoman by ignoring her pain and anguish. For instance, on the topic of master-on-slave rape, Stampp noted, "For many white men the problem was not so simple. Often the matter weighed heavy upon their consciences long after the affair had ended."[18] Similarly, Genovese wrote, "Typically, the slaveholders could not take their black 'wenches' without suffering psychic agony . . . ."[19] As we will see, some slaveholders who raped or ordered the rape of their bondswomen were unburdened by conscience.

Bondswoman as Promiscuous Collaborator

Other American historians offer the false premise that the majority of bondswomen willingly accommodated their owners with sex because they regarded sexual contact with white men as a privilege. For instance, Leslie Howard Owens would have us believe that a significant number of bondswomen "willingly mixed their blood with that of the planters, and did not try to disguise the fact."[20] Consequently, these scholars sanction the sexual assault of black bondswomen by unfairly depicting them as promiscuous collaborators in their own victimization.[21]

Notes

1. *Merriam-Webster OnLine Dictionary*, <www.m-w.com/cgi-bin/dictionary> (18 Feb. 2006).

2. Susan Brownmiller, *Against Our Will* (New York: Bantam Books, 1975), 8.

3. Thomas D. Morris, *Southern Slavery and the Law 1619-1860* (Chapel Hill: University of North Carolina Press, 1996), 306.

4. William Goodell, *The American Slave Code in Theory and Practice: Its Distinctive Features Shown by Its Statutes, Judicial Decisions, and Illustrative Facts* (New York: American and Foreign Anti-Slavery Society, 1853), part 1, ch. 4, 86.

5. Mrs. A. M. French, *Slavery in South Carolina and the Ex-slaves; or, The Port Royal Mission* (New York: Winchell M. French, 1862; reprinted New York: Negro Universities Press, 1969), 137.

6. Peter Kolchin, *American Slavery 1619-1877* (New York: Hill and Wang, 1993), 124-25.

7. Kenneth M. Stampp, *The Peculiar Institution: Slavery in the Ante-Bellum South* (New York: Vintage Books, 1956), 196, 350-60.

8. E. Franklin Frazier, *The Negro Family in the United States* (Chicago: University of Chicago Press, 1939), 116-17.

9. Leslie Howard Owens, *This Species of Property* (New York: Oxford University Press, Inc., 1976), 211-12.

10. Robert W. Fogel and Stanley L. Engerman, *Time on the Cross* (Boston: Little, Brown & Co., 1974), 130-33.

11. John C. Perry, *Myths & Realities of American Slavery* (Shippensburg, Pa.: Burd Street Press, 2002), 127.

12. Angela Y. Davis, *Women, Race & Class* (New York: Vintage Books, 1983), 175.

13. Eugene D. Genovese, *Roll Jordan Roll: The World the Slaves Made* (New York: Vintage Books, 1972), 415-39.

14. John W. Blassingame, *The Slave Community: Plantation Life in the Ante-*

Bellum South, rev. and expanded (Cary, North Carolina: Oxford University Press, 1979), 154.

15. Blassingame, *The Slave Community*, 154.

16. Kenneth Stampp wrote, "Evidence . . . suggests that human behavior in the Old South was very human indeed, that sexual contacts between the races were not rare aberrations of a small group of depraved whites but a frequent occurrence involving whites of all social and cultural levels." Stampp, *The Peculiar Institution*, 350.

17. For example, Eugene D. Genovese wrote, "Many white men who began by taking a slave girl in an act of sexual exploitation ended by loving her and the children she bore. They were not supposed to, but they did . . . . White men slept with black women . . . and much more often than they were supposed to, those who began by seeking casual pleasure ended by caring." Genovese, *Roll Jordan Roll*, 415-18.

18. Stampp, *The Peculiar Institution*, 357.

19. Genovese, *Roll Jordan Roll*, 424.

20. Owens, *This Species of Property*, 197, 211.

21. For example, E. Franklin Frazier wrote the following:

In many instances, men of the master race did not meet much resistance on the part of the slave woman. The mere prestige of the white race was sufficient to secure compliance with their desires. . . .There were often certain concrete advantages to be gained by surrendering themselves to men of the master race that overcame any moral scruples these women might have had . . . . Material attraction played a part in securing compliance of the women . . . . It appears that, aside from the prestige of the white race and the material advantages to be gained, these women were as responsive to the attractiveness of the white males as the latter were to the charm of slave women.

Frazier, *The Negro Family in the United States*, 54-55.

CHAPTER NINE

Master-on-Slave Rape Revealed

The historians Nathan Irvin Huggins, Peter Kolchin, and David Brion Davis are non-participants in the concealment the slaveholders' acts of rape. Although Huggins said that white men were never really prohibited from "finding their pleasure with black women," he did call the act rape.[1] He wrote,

> They were unequal encounters in which the source of power was never forgotten . . . . The strategies were simple: get her away, alone—in a room, the pantry, the barn, an isolated field—some pretext, any order. The game would begin: first playful, jovial, pleading, and suggestive; then losing patience, becoming direct and commanding. She might plead, laugh, resist, fight him off. But sooner or later it would happen. Perhaps it would be brutal, she falling back, taking his body into hers, whimpering and swallowing her hurt. Once it was over she could walk away ashamed, not because she was prudish or coy, but because her private self had been defiled. This pain would last for a long time to come . . . . *Rape is always the same.* But the game was not always so. . . . Black women had little choice in the matter if white men set out to take them.[2] (emphasis mine)

We should give credit to Peter Kolchin as well for candidly noting that, far more often, "slaves who had sex with whites did so against their will, whether victims of outright rape or of the powerlessness that made resistance to advances futile and the use of force in such advances unnecessary."[3] He correctly concluded that casual emotionless sex between captor and captive was "a routine feature of life on many, perhaps most, slaveholdings" and "caused anguish to black women."[4] David Brion Davis, perhaps the most forthright male historian on this topic, noted that he found "abundant evidence that many slaveowners, sons of slaveowners, and overseers . . . in effect raped the wives and daughters of slave families." Davis added that the ubiquity of white-on-black rape in the ante-bellum South "was sufficient to deeply scar and humiliate black women, to instill rage in black men, and to arouse both shame and bitterness in white women."[5] His candor is commendable.

As Huggins and Kolchin do, the historians Gerda Lerner and Susan Brownmiller have a clearer understanding of the power dynamic of the master-slave sexual encounter—as both knew the bondswoman was powerless to resist her master's sexual advances. Gerda Lerner acknowledged that the rape of black women by white men was "so widespread as to be general . . . always possible and *could in no way be fought or avoided.*"[6] Similarly, the feminist historian Susan Brownmiller forcefully argued that the black woman's body, "and all of its parts, belonged outright to her master . . . the knife, the whip and the gun [were] always there to be used against her."[7] To varying degrees, the typical bondswoman tried to resist her owner's sexual advances, but in most instances her master engaged in sexual intercourse with her forcibly, or at least by threatening physical injury; in short, he raped her.

Rape as an Act of Counter-Insurgency

At a time when books written by such feminists as Susan Brownmiller and others have long since clarified our understanding of rape, most American historians writing on this topic during the last thirty years have not benefited from their work. They fail or refuse to recognize master-on-slave rape as a violent act and a way of destroying the bondswoman's will to resist. Instead, they often romanticize the violent encounter—mischaracterizing it as an irrepressible act of love, lust, or desire.

Master-on-slave rape was often not a random act of violence; it was planned and pre-meditated.[8] It was a political act as well, or what the historian Angela Davis called "an unveiled element of counter-insurgency," essential to the white man's subjugation of a people for economic and psychological gain. The slaveholder's rape of the bondswoman was one of various means of physical and psychological control. If rape, in Brownmiller's words, "is nothing more or less than a conscious process of intimidation by which all men keep all women in fear," it should not surprise us that the slaveholder tried to destroy the black bondswoman's proclivity toward resistance by raping her. [9]

Notes

1. Nathan Irvin Huggins, *Black Odyssey: The Afro-American Ordeal in Slavery* (New York: Pantheon Books, 1977), 117.

2. Huggins, *Black Odyssey*, 141-43.

3. Peter Kolchin, *American Slavery 1619-1877* (New York: Hill and Wang, 1993), 124-25.

4. Kolchin, *American Slavery*, 125.

5. David Brion Davis, *Inhuman Bondage: The Rise and Fall of Slavery in the New World* (New York: Oxford University Press, 2006), 201.

6. Gerda Lerner, *Black Women in White America* (New York: Vintage Books, 1972), 46. (emphasis mine)

7. Susan Brownmiller, *Against Our Will* (New York: Bantam Books, 1975), 166.
8. Brownmiller, *Against Our Will*, 8.
9. Brownmiller, *Against Our Will*, 8.

CHAPTER TEN

The Threat of Injury or Death

The slave codes of the ante-bellum South did not inquire into the cause or specific reason for the murder of a slave. As Reverend William Goodell explained in 1853, laws permitting an owner or overseer to murder his slave required only that the slave disobeyed that owner or overseer.[1] What then were the consequences for the many bondswomen who resisted their masters' and overseers' sexual advances? We know that the slave codes prevented them from testifying against whites, and that no white man could ever rape a black woman under Southern law. Goodell observed that the legal relationship of master and bondswoman gave the master "unlimited control and full possession of her own person, and forb[ade] her on pain of death . . . to resist him, if he drag[ged] her to his bed!"[2] Thus, the bondswoman gave up her body under the threat of injury or death because she knew that both her owner and her overseer could lawfully take her life for disobeying any command.

White men raped free black women in the ante-bellum South as well. A speaker at the North Carolina Constitutional Convention of 1835 told the audience, "A white man may go into the house of a free black, maltreat and abuse him and commit any outrage upon his family, for all of which the laws cannot reach him, unless some white person saw the act."[3] The Louisiana ex-slave Rosa Mattox summed up that disturbing consequence of the slave codes. She said, "I can tell you that a white man laid a nigger gal whenever he wanted her."[4]

If the resolute bondswoman—intent on protecting her virtue—found blandishments or gifts unpersuasive, the slaveholder who was determined to rape her often kept his bullwhip within arm's reach to convince her otherwise.[5] One traveler observed an incident in which a slaveowner demanded sexual intercourse of a bondswoman who resisted his command. The traveler noted that she was flogged repeatedly, after which, "seeing that her case was hopeless," gave herself up to be the victim of rape.[6] In the following excerpt from his narrative, Henry Bibb gives an account of another slaveholder who forced his slave-girl to have sexual relations with his son by torturing her with the lash:

I heard the deacon tell one of the slave girls that he had bought her for a wife for his boy Stephen, which office he compelled her fully to perform against her will. This he enforced by a threat. At first, the poor girl neglected to do this, having no sort of affection for the man—but she was finally forced to it by the application of the driver's lash.[7]

The bondswomen who lived in the big house were most vulnerable to sexual assault by their owners. "Prophet" John Henry Kemp, a mulatto ex-slave from Florida, related the story of his mother, Arnette Young. The house slave of the slaveholder John Gay, she was in such paralyzing fear of being raped by her master that she complained to his wife. Young informed Gay's wife that her husband was constantly seeking her for a mistress and threatening her with death if she did not submit, but Mrs. Gay's response gave Young no comfort. She replied, "My husband is a dirty man and will find some reason to kill you if you don't. I can't do a thing with him." Unfortunately working under the same roof and in close quarters with John Gay, Arnette Young was forced under threat of death to submit to him; he raped her. Her son "Prophet" John Henry Kemp—born of that heinous act—lived to tell us about it.[8] The ex-slave Linda Brent (writing under the pseudonym Harriet Brent Jacobs) noted that she was forced to live under the same roof with her master where he, a man forty years her elder, "daily violat[ed] the most sacred commandments of nature."[9] Where could she have turned for protection?

Mindful that slaveholders were accustomed to raping young slave-women, the Texas ex-slave Betty Powers, a small child when America legally abolished slavery, said,

Dey thinks nothin' on de plantation 'bout de feelins of de women and dere ain't no spect for dem. De overseer and white men do de women like dey wants to. De women better not make no fuss 'bout sich. If she do, it am de whippin' for her. I sho' thanks de Lawd surrender done come befo' I's old 'nough to have to stand for sich.[10]

Although most former slaves were reluctant to discuss the matter or to dwell upon it in their narratives, some talked openly about how their owners raped them or their family members, or how they were beaten—some severely—for resisting the masters' sexual advances. For example, Martha Allen, a former slave from North Carolina, recalled a young master who wanted to have sexual intercourse with her mother, but her mother told him no. Allen said, "So he chunks a lightwood knot an' hits her on de haid wid it."[11] Frequently tied and beaten viciously by her owner in an effort to subdue her pride, the ex-slave Elizabeth Keckley revealed that those savage efforts were not the only thing that caused her pain and anguish during her residence on a Hillsboro, North Carolina plantation. She wrote the following:

For four years a white man—I spare the world his name—had base designs upon me. I do not care to dwell upon this subject, for it is one that is fraught with pain. Suffice it to say, that he persecuted me for four years, and I became a mother.[12]

Referring to her child, Keckley added,

The child of which, he was the father was the only child that I ever brought into the world. If my poor boy ever suffered any humiliating pangs on account of birth, he could not blame his mother, for God knows that she did not wish to give him life; he must blame the edicts of that society which deemed it no crime to undermine the virtue of girls in my position.[13]

The fugitive slave John Thompson noted in his autobiography that when his sister resisted her master's sexual overture, the angered slaveholder ordered the girl beaten "until the blood stood in puddles under her feet." This became a recurring event.[14] Apparently sold for her beauty, a quinteroon[15] bondswoman named Delia Clarke was whipped savagely by her new owner—in sight of her brother and mother—because she rebuffed the owner's indecent proposal. The disappointed slaveholder sold her to a New Orleans brothel.[16]

In his narrative, the South Carolina ex-slave Cureton Milling describes the circumstances under which his master raped his aunt:

He take 'vantage of the young gal slaves. "Yo go yonder and shell corn in the crib," he say to one of them. He's the master so she have to go. Then he send the others to work some other place, then would go to the crib. He did this to my very aunt and she had a mulatto boy.[17]

The threat of physical injury or death came from the overseers as well. Minnie Fulkes told us that one overseer whipped her mother mercilessly until the blood ran down her back and heels and bathed her in salt and water because she refused to have sexual intercourse with him. Fulkes said, "Mind you, now mama's marster didn't know dis wuz going on. You know . . . if slaves would tell, why dem overseers would kill 'em."[18] Fannie Berry, a former slave from Virginia, also recalled that bondswomen "would be beat up so when dey resisted, an' sometimes if you'll 'helled de overseer would kill yo'." She concluded, "Us colored women had to go through a plenty, I tell you."[19] Most slaves understood the trying situation through which a bondswoman endured and would not have pointed an accusatory finger at her because of her predicament.

Child Rape

Rape is also defined as unlawful sexual activity carried out with a person who is beneath a certain age—sometimes called child rape or statutory rape.[20] Though it is a further and stronger indictment of the slaveholding class, we should know that slaveholders raped slave-children. The historian Deborah Gray White explained that the root of much of a slave-mother's anxiety was her fear that her young daughter would be raped. She observed, "In the long run, however, a mother could do little but hope that her daughter made it through adolescence and young womanhood unscathed by sexual abuse."[21]

Linda Brent recalled that the initiation of a slave-girl began at an early age. "When she is fourteen or fifteen," wrote Brent, "her owner or his sons or the overseer or perhaps all of them begin to bribe her with presents. If these fail to accomplish their purpose, she is whipped or starved into submission to their will."[22] Apparently, Ben Simpson's sister, Emma, was raped and impregnated at the age of fourteen. Simpson said that her master "sold her when she's 'bout fifteen, jus' befo' her baby was born."[23]

Lewis Brown, a former slave from Mississippi, also saw masters and overseers catching young black girls and whipping them to make them do what they wanted.[24] Mollie Kinsey remembered one slaveholder who forced her sister, "just a small girl," to "go out and lay on the table, and two or three white men would have intercourse with her before they'd let her get up."[25] In the ante-bellum South, unless they died a martyr's death, innumerable adolescent slave-girls became the victims of rape.[26]

Notes

1. William Goodell, *The American Slave Code in Theory and Practice: Its Distinctive Features Shown by Its Statutes, Judicial Decisions, and Illustrative Facts* (New York: American and Foreign Anti-Slavery Society, 1853), part 1, ch. 12, 257.

2. Goodell, *The American Slave Code,* part. 1, ch. 7, 108.

3. Arthur W. Calhoun, *A Social History of the American Family from Colonial Times to the Present,* vol. 2 (Cleveland: The Arthur H. Clark Co., 1917), 291.

4. James Mellon, ed., *Bullwhip Days: The Slaves Remember* (New York: Avon Books, 1990), 122.

5. Calhoun, *A Social History of the American Family,* 292.

6. Rev. Theodore D. Weld, et al, ed., *Slavery as It Is: Testimony of a Thousand Witnesses* (New York: American Anti-Slavery Society, 1839), 15.

7. Henry Bibb, *Narrative of the Life and Adventures of Henry Bibb, an American Slave* (New York: H. Bibb, 1849), 199.

8. *Born in Slavery: Slave Narratives from the Federal Writers' Project, 1936-1938* (Wash., D.C.: Library of Congress, 2001), Florida Narratives, vol. 3, 186. <memory.loc.gov/ammem/snhtml/snhome> (15 April 2006).

9. Harriet Brent Jacobs, *Incidents in the Life of a Slave Girl*, ed. L. Maria Child (Boston: Act of Congress, 1861), 44-45.

10. George P. Rawick, ed., *The American Slave: A Composite Autobiography*, 41 vols. (Westport, Conn.: Greenwood Publishing Co., 1972), Texas, part 3, 191-92.

11. *Born in Slavery: Slave Narratives from the Federal Writers' Project,* North Carolina Narratives, vol. 11, part 1, 14.

12. Elizabeth Keckley, *Behind the Scenes* (New York: Carleton & Co. Publishers, 1868), 38.

13. Keckley, *Behind the Scenes*, 38.

14. John Thompson, *The Life of John Thompson, A Fugitive Slave: Containing His History of Twenty-Five Years in Bondage and His Providential Escape, Written by Himself* (Worcester: J. Thompson, 1856), 103-09.

15. Her father was a Scotchman and her mother was a "quadroon." She had a mere drop of African blood in her veins. Francis William Newman, *Character of the Southern States* (Manchester, England: Union and Emancipation Depot, 1863), 7.

16. Newman, *Character of the Southern States*, 7.

17. *Born in Slavery: Slave Narratives from the Federal Writers' Project*, South Carolina Narratives, vol. 14, part 3, 194.

18. *Born in Slavery: Slave Narratives from the Federal Writers' Project*, Virginia Narratives, vol. 17, 11.

19. *Born in Slavery: Slave Narratives from the Federal Writers' Project*, Virginia Narratives, vol. 17, 2.

20. "Sexual intercourse with a person who is below the statutory age of consent." *Merriam-Webster On-Line Dictionary* <www.m-w.com/cgi-bin/dictionary> (18 Feb. 2006).

21. Deborah Gray White, *Ar'n't I a Woman?: Female Slaves in the Plantation South* (New York: W. W. Norton & Co., 1985), 95-96.

22. Jacobs, *Incidents in the Life of a Slave Girl*, 79.

23. *Born in Slavery: Slave Narratives from the Federal Writers' Project*, Texas Narratives, vol. 16, part 4, 28. Although it is clear from Simpson's testimony that his sister was raped by her master, it is not clear who fathered her child.

24. *Born in Slavery: Slave Narratives from the Federal Writers' Project*, Arkansas Narratives, vol. 2, part 1, 293.

25. Andrew Waters, ed., *On Jordan's Stormy Banks* (Winston-Salem, N.C.: John F. Blair, Publisher, 2000), 20.

26. Calhoun, *A Social History of the American Family*, 294.

CHAPTER ELEVEN

Slave Resistance

Despite the likelihood of bodily harm and sometimes death, brave bonds-men tried to protect their wives from sexual assault. For example, the ex-slave W. H. Robinson's father once told him that he had hidden out in the woods eleven months after trying to protect his wife from his master.[1] The former slave Josiah Henson's father was whipped and his ear cropped off for striking an overseer who attempted to rape his wife.[2] Some white men must have realized nonetheless that sexual encounters with their bondswomen could be dangerous. As Deborah Gray White noted, enraged black men occasionally "mustered suicidal courage" and killed them for such acts.[3] For raping his wife, one slave named Ben shot and killed a white man named Joseph Good-ing. Ben was determined to take his master's gun out of the house where it generally stood loaded, pursue Gooding, and shoot him. That he did.[4]

White Southerners, however, publicly executed bondsmen who killed white men in defense of their slave-wives. In 1836, a visitor to Mississippi recorded an incident of a slave who murdered a white man who owned him. The visitor made a written note of the fact that the white man owned the slave's wife as well and was in the habit of sleeping with her. Her slave-husband confessed that he had killed his master because of it, and he believed that he was going to be rewarded in heaven for it. Indeed, that act cost the black man his life. He was burned at the stake, beheaded, and his head stuck on a pole for public display.[5] Slaveholders tortured, mutilated, and frequently killed black men for coming to the defense of their mates. For the bondsman, standing up to the master in defense of the bondswoman's virtue was tanta-mount to committing suicide.

Inasmuch as the bondsmen were as powerless as the bondswomen, the women were sometimes as inclined to defend themselves as the men were to defend them. The Maryland ex-slave Richard Macks told us about one mulatto slave-woman of fine stature and good looks who was put up for sale. She was of such high spirits and determined disposition that when a slave trader purchased her and attempted to rape her, she grabbed a knife and castrated him. He died the next day from the injury. Although charged with murder, atypically, she was fortunate enough to have been protected by Union troops and ultimately taken to Washington, D.C. where she was freed.[6]

In 1850, Robert Newsom, a white Missouri farmer and grandfather over sixty years of age, purchased a fourteen-year-old slave-girl named Celia and raped her as he took her home. In fact, the slaveholder impregnated Celia three times during her teenaged years. Ill during her third pregnancy and fed up with being raped, on June 23, 1855, Celia warned Newsom that she would hurt him if he tried to rape her again. Subsequently, Newsom went down to Celia's cabin one night and attempted to rape her, but armed with a stick, she struck him twice, killing him. She then burned his body in her fireplace and spread his ashes outside. When the town discovered the murder of her master, Celia was tried, convicted of first-degree murder, and ordered executed by hanging. Ironically, the town delayed her execution until December 21, 1855 so that she could give birth to the property of her master's estate, but the child was still-born.[7]

The practice of delaying the execution of pregnant slaves until the birth of their babies was not unique. Charity Morris, an ex-slave from Arkansas, told us the story of her pregnant cousin Sallie. Sallie murdered an evil master named Jim not only because he habitually beat her and other slaves, but also because he locked them up until sunrise when they returned home from the field each night. Lying in wait for her master, Sallie cracked him in the head with a poker. With the help of another slave named "Little" Joe, she put his head in her fireplace. An investigation of her owner's death revealed his blood on Sallie's under dress. Although Sallie was tried and convicted of murder, Morris said that her execution by hanging was delayed until she gave birth to her baby.[8]

Lucy, another slave, resisted the sexual advances of her white owner and successfully plotted with her slave lover, Frank, to murder him. Both Lucy and Frank were hanged at the public gallows, and according to Charles Ball, "There were at least fifteen thousand people present at this scene, more than half of whom were black; all the masters, for a great distance round the country, having compelled their people to come to this hanging."[9] For the bondswoman who killed the slaveholder—even in defense of her virtue—white vengeance was swift and certain.

Notes

1. W. H. Robinson, *From Log Cabin to the Pulpit* (Eau Claire, Wis., 1913), 25.
2. Josiah Henson, *The Life of Josiah Henson* (Boston, 1849), 67.
3. Deborah Gray White, *Ar'n't I a Woman?: Female Slaves in the Plantation South* (New York: W. W. Norton & Co., 1985), 146.
4. Executive Papers, Archives of Virginia Letters received January 12, 1801, as

quoted in James Hugh Johnson's *Race Relations in Virginia and Miscegenation in the South 1776-1860* (Amherst: University of Massachusetts Press, 1970), 305.

5. Rev. Theodore D. Weld, et al, ed., *Slavery as It Is: Testimony of a Thousand Witnesses,* (New York: American Anti-Slavery Society, 1839), 157.

6. *Born in Slavery: Slave Narratives from the Federal Writers' Project, 1936-1938* (Wash., D.C.: Library of Congress, 2001), Maryland Narratives, vol. 8, 53. <memory.loc.gov/ammem/snhtml/snhome> (15 April 2006).

7. A. Leon Higginbotham, Jr., *Shades of Freedom: Racial Politics and Presumptions of the American Legal Process* (New York: Oxford University Press, 1996), 99-101; David Brion Davis, *Inhuman Bondage: The Rise and Fall of Slavery in the New World* (New York: Oxford University Press, 2006), 201-02.

8. *Born in Slavery: Slave Narratives from the Federal Writers' Project,* Arkansas Narratives, vol. 2, part 5, 149-50.

9. Charles Ball, *Slavery in the United States: A Narrative of the Life and Adventures of Charles Ball, a Black Man, Who Lived Forty Years in Maryland, South Carolina and Georgia, as a Slave* (Lewistown, Pa.: J. W. Shugert, 1836), 295.

Chapter Twelve

Rape and Slave Breeding

In 1790, the black population in the United States numbered a little more than 750,000. Almost 89% of that population lived in the South Atlantic states where the greatest demand for black labor existed.[1] But notwithstanding the Atlantic Slave Trade's official end on January 1, 1808, the slave population increased nearly fourfold between the years 1810 and 1860.[2] During that same period, average prime slave prices (which fluctuated with the price of cotton) rose from $900 to $1,600.[3] The conventional explanation offered by many American slavery historians for the exceptional rate of slave population growth is that it was natural—due to an equal ratio of female to male slaves,[4] less grueling working conditions relative to those in other parts of the Americas, and the slaves' so-called promiscuity. With the notable exception of John Hope Franklin, historians generally attribute little, if any, of the increase in the slave population during that period to the slaveholders' practice of slave breeding.[5] The master's rape of the bondswoman, however, was not merely an act of counter-insurgency; it was a profit-making phenomenon. By forcibly impregnating his bondswoman, the slaveholder increased the size of his slave labor force.

Kenneth Stampp believed that systematic slave breeding was unlikely. He found scant available evidence of it.[6] But Franklin not only acknowledged "that innumerable slaveholders deliberately undertook to increase the number of saleable slaves by advantageously mating them," he called the ante-bellum South's practice of slave breeding "one of the most fantastic manipulations of human development in the history of mankind."[7] Slave breeding did occur. Absolute control of the bondswoman's reproductive schedule meant a steady supply of slave-babies. Slaveowners compelled their bondswomen, married or unmarried, to bear children. One slaveholder reported that in the states of North Carolina, Virginia, Maryland, Kentucky, Tennessee, and Missouri as much attention was paid to the breeding and growth of black slaves as to that of horses and mules. He noted that slaveowners further south raised them for their own use and for the market.[8]

Slaveholders measured a bondswoman's value by her physical strength, her portliness, and—most important—the number of healthy children she bore. The master purchased young bondswomen, expecting his slave population to increase rapidly. He found in slave breeding one of the more effective ways of increasing his agricultural capital. On August 20, 1849, for instance, the Texas slaveholder Alva Fitzpatrick penned a letter to his nephew, giving him the following instructions:

> Get as many young negro women as you can. Get as many cows as you can .
> . . . It is the greatest country for an increase that I . . . ever saw in my life. I have been [here] six years and I have had fifteen negro children born and last year three more young negro women commenced breeding which will add seven born last year and five of them is living and doing well . . . . [A]ttend to the foregoing instructions and in ten or fifteen or twenty years you will do as well as any man in this or any other country.[9]

A former slave from Georgia, Isiah Green, told us that large slave families were the aim and pride of the slaveholder, who quickly learned which of his bondswomen bore children and which did not. Green said, "A greedy owner got rid of those who didn't breed."[10] Berry Clay, though never a slave, recalled that the master demanded that his bondswoman be fruitful. As did Green, he said, "A barren woman was separated from her husband and usually sold."[11] In fact, the Arkansas ex-slave Mary Brown's grandmother was sold for that reason. As a young woman, she bore no children. A firm conviction that she was barren—damaged goods—led her owner to sell her to a slaveholder named Mr. Taylor. Perhaps determined not to be sold again, Brown's grandmother subsequently bore eleven children, but Taylor sold them all away from her for financial gain.[12] Although many bondswomen were fearful of being sold, their fecundity sometimes brought them—if not their children—at least some measure of security against it.[13]

As mentioned previously, generally rape statutes did not protect young slave-girls in the South in the way they protected young white girls. In 1857, the Mississippi legislature made it a capital offense for a slave to have "carnal connection" with any white girl under the age of fourteen.[14] That law, and similar laws enacted throughout the ante-bellum South, afforded black girls—slaves and free—no protection. Consequently, not a few slave-girls were impregnated as soon as they reached puberty. Deborah Gray White maintained that bondswomen typically bore their first children at the age of nineteen—two years younger than the age at which Southern white women generally had their first children.[15] But writing in 1919, the women's suffrage advocate Rebecca L. Felton noted that because frequent births of slave-babies were very profitable for the slaveholder, slave childbearing sometimes began at twelve years of age.[16] The North Carolina ex-slave Hilliard Yellerday said as well that slave-girls were expected to have children as soon as they were capable; "some of them had children at the age of twelve and thirteen years old."[17]

The slaveholder assigned a higher market value to young childbearing bondswomen because they brought him more wealth in the form of slave-babies. The North Carolina ex-slave Fannie Moore in fact stated, "De 'breed woman' always bring more money den de rest, even de men. When dey put her on the block dey put all her chillen around her to show folks how fast she can have chillen."[18] Coming across a slave auction on his journey through Memphis, Tennessee, a former slave from Arkansas, Boston Blackwell, saw a young slave-woman of childbearing age bid off for $1,500. He also said, "They always brought good money."[19] Isiah Green opined, "A slave trader could always sell a breeding woman for twice the usual amount."[20]

Fertile young slave-girls, each commanding as much as a thousand dollars or more on the auction block, were expected by their masters to bear healthy slave-children as early as possible and at least once every two years thereafter. Slave traders placed advertisements in newspapers throughout the South, emphasizing their reproductive qualities. In one instance on May 16, 1838, a leading political paper of South Carolina, the *Charleston Mercury,* ran an advertisement for the sale of one young slave-woman raised in Virginia and her two little girls, describing the bondswoman as "remarkably strong and healthy," "very prolific in her generating qualities," and naturally providing "a rare opportunity to any person who wishes to raise a family of healthy servants for [his] own use."[21]

Realizing the great demand for slave labor and fearful that this labor supply would soon become exhausted, white Southerners who had sufficient funds purchased fertile young slave-girls, believing that they were sound investments because slaveholders demanded and received fruitful returns.[22] Deborah Gray White found black men's and black women's American experiences as slaves equally severe, but she underscored the most significant difference between the two: the women were compelled by their masters to bear and nurture slave-children.[23] White also pointed out, "In the pre-Civil War period black women were very prolific. According to demographers the crude birth-rate exceeded fifty per one thousand, meaning that each year more than one fifth of the black women in the 15-to-44 age cohort bore a child."[24] One of the more prolific childbearing bondswomen, the grandmother of the Arkansas ex-slave Josephine Howell gave birth to twenty-one children. Howell said that her grandmother's fecundity made her very valuable to her owner.[25] The former slave Tempie Herndon, 103 years old when interviewed, said that she was "worth a heap to Marse George" because she had so many "muley strong and healthy" children.[26]

About bondswomen's childbearing duties, Susan Brownmiller wrote the following:

> [They] were expected to "breed"; some were retained expressly for that purpose. In the lexicon of slavery, "breeder woman," "childbearing woman," "too old to breed" and "not a breeding woman" were common descriptive terms. In country breeding was crucial to the planter economy after the Afri-

can slave trade was banned . . . and the slave woman's value increased in accordance with her ability to produce healthy offspring. Domestic production of slave babies for sale to other slave states became a small industry in the fertile upper South . . . . The state of Virginia annually exported between six thousand and twenty thousand homegrown slaves to the deeper South where the land, the climate and the harsher workload took precedence over fecundity. The Virginia-reared slave, like Virginia leaf tobacco, was always in great demand.[27]

In many instances, the slaveholder paired the slave-girl with a mate of his choosing and ordered her to bear children, particularly when he owned both slaves. John Perry found it very rare, and Deborah Gray White maintained that it was atypical for a slaveowner to assign a male slave to a female slave and demand that they have slave-children.[28] When Adella S. Dixon interviewed eighty-nine-year-old Berry Clay in 1936, however, his recall of the slaveholder's general practice was to the contrary. Clay told us that the master selected the bondswoman's husband and "only in rare occasions was the desire of the individual considered."[29]

Many ex-slaves had similar recollections. For example, a former slave from Texas, Jacob Branch stated, "Massa go buy a cullud man name Uncle Charley Fenner . . . brung him to the quarters and say, 'Renee, here you husband,' and den turn to Uncle and say, 'Charley, dis your woman.' Den dey consider dem married. Dat the way dey marry den, by de massa's word."[30] Betty Powers also told us, "Dem times, cullud folk am jus' put together. De massa say, 'Jim and Nancy, you go live together,' and when that order give, it better be done."[31] The Arkansas ex-slave Virginia "Jennie" Davis said that a slaveowner put her aunt Eliza and her aunt's husband together.[32] One observer of slave auctions, the Texas ex-slave Jordan Smith, recalled that the slave buyer would manhandle the bondswoman to determine her physical strength. Once convinced that she was a good "breeder," he would purchase her and pair her with a total stranger for childbearing purposes. Smith said,

> They lined the women up on one side and the men on the other. A buyer would walk up and down 'tween the two rows and grab a woman and try to throw her down and feel of her to see how she's put up. If she's purty strong, he'd say, "Is she a good breeder?" If the gal was eighteen or nineteen and put up good she was worth 'bout fifteen hundred dollars. Then the buyer'd pick out a strong, young nigger boy about the same age and buy him. When he got home he'd say to them, "I want you two to stay together. I want young niggers."[33]

Slaveholders loaned their bondswomen to masters on neighboring plantations for childbearing purposes as well. J. W. Whitfield, a former slave from Arkansas, said, "If a landowner had a girl and another wanted that girl for one of his men, they would give him her to wife."[34] When the North Carolina ex-slave Willie McCullough's mother turned the age of sixteen, her owner went to a local slaveholder, picked out a six-foot tall black man—almost an entire stranger to her—and ordered her to marry him. McCullough said that her master introduced several different men to her "just about the same as if she had been a cow."[35] Hilliard Yellerday similarly said that slaveholders would sometimes borrow large, six-foot tall "hale hearty" black men from nearby plantations for their young slave-girls.

Adolescent slave-girls were required to receive the attentions of men of their owners' choice even though some of them loved someone else. Yellerday told us, "This was a general custom."[36] In that situation, the bondswoman had no reproductive rights that her master was bound to respect. She had no control over her body; her childbearing decisions were guided not by her will, but rather by her owner's will.

In 1847, William Wells Brown gave an account of the slaveholder John Calvert and his young slave-woman Lavinia. Calvert sold away Lavinia's fiancé and demanded that she pick another husband for childbearing purposes, but she resolved not to marry any other man. According to Brown, "Mr. Calvert whipped her in such a manner that it was thought that she would die."[37] Engaged to a young man from a neighboring plantation, another bondswoman found out about her master's intention to pair her arbitrarily with a male slave of his choosing, but she would not have it so. The fugitive slave John Brown noted, "In fear and desperation, she made a strike for freedom."[38] We do not know whether or not she obtained her freedom. No doubt, her owner was determined to secure her capture.

Primarily economic considerations influenced the slaveholder's choice of mates for his slaves. Would the paired slaves beget stout, healthy offspring—physically prepared for a life of incessant and arduous toil? Katie Darling said that her master would "pick out a portly man and a portly gal and just put 'em together" because he wanted the "stock."[39] Some masters would reserve the slave-child born of that pair for breeding purposes if he was healthy and robust, but J. W. Whitfield recalled that if the child was "puny and sickly, they were not bothered about him."[40] The ninety-seven-year-old Missouri ex-slave Bill Simms remembered as well that neighboring plantation owners would ask a big strong bondsman to come over and see their slave-women, hoping that he might want to marry one of them. As did Whitfield, Simms told us that certain slaveholders did not want small black men marrying their bondswomen because those owners "valued their slaves . . . only for what they could do, just like they would horses."[41]

Some slaveholders amassed great wealth by breeding slaves solely for the market. Charlotte Martin was owned by a very cruel master named Judge Wilkerson. He found it very profitable to breed and sell slaves. Martin said,

> He selected the strongest and best male and female slaves and mated them exclusively for breeding. The huskiest babies were given the best of attention in order that they might grow into sturdy youths, for it was those who brought the highest prices at the slave markets.[42]

Louisa "Nor" Everett, a ninety-year-old ex-slave nicknamed after her birthplace of Norfolk, Virginia, not only recalled that her owner bred slaves; she told her story of how she and her ex-slave husband, Sam Everett, met as slave-children on "Big Jim" McClain's plantation. An evil master, Big Jim McClain owned over one hundred slaves. Louisa Everett said that he mated his slaves indiscriminately and without regard for family unions. If he thought a certain pair of slaves might have strong healthy babies, he would force them to have sexual relations—even though they were married to other slaves. If there was any reluctance on their part, Big Jim—bullwhip over his shoulder—would force them to have sex in his presence. He employed the same tactic if he thought a certain slave-couple was not producing children fast enough. Everett said that Big Jim McClain took pleasure in watching his slaves have sex and "often entertained his friends in this manner." [43]

Slaveholders made it very clear to their young bondswomen that they were expected to bear healthy slave-children. Although some masters offered rewards such as calico dresses and silver dollars to prolific slave-women, others obtained the desired result through the threat of torture or sale. In the following excerpt from her narrative, Louisa "Nor" Everett describes the lewd manner in which her owner forced her upon her slave-husband, Sam:

> Marse Jim called me and Sam ter him and ordered Sam to pull off his shirt—that was all the McClain niggers wore—and he said to me: "Nor, do you think you can stand this big nigger?" He had that old bullwhip flung acrost his shoulder, and Lawd, that man could hit so hard! So I jes' said "yassur, I guess so," and tried to hide my face so I couldn't see Sam's nakedness, but he made me look at him anyhow. Well, he told us what we must git busy and do in his presence, and we had to do it. After that we was considered man and wife. Me and Sam was a healthy pair and had fine big babies, so I never had another man forced on me, thank God. Sam was kind to me and I learned to love him. [44]

Some slaveholders reserved healthy and physically robust adult male slaves solely for breeding purposes. For example, Willie Williams, a former slave from Louisiana, said that his owner was anxious to raise big slaves—individuals who were able to perform "lots of work and sell for a heap of money." His master owned ten big, strong bondswomen who were not allowed to get married. Instead, a doctor examined the women and a robust male slave, and their owner ordered them to replenish his plantation with healthy young slave labor. Williams stated, "Dat nigger do no work but watch dem womens and he am de husband for dem all. De marster sho' was a-raisin' some fine niggers dat way." [45] The father of Arkansas ex-slave Oscar Felix Junell, Peter W. Junell, told him that the slaveholders took the finest and portliest looking black men for breeding purposes. He also testified that, "They wouldn't let them strain themselves up nor nothin' like that. They wouldn't make them do much hard work." [46]

Other former bondsmen revealed that their fathers were breeding slaves. Barney Stone, for example, informed us that his father, "Buck" Grant, a "buck slave" on the slaveholder John Grant's plantation, "was used as a male cow is used on the stock farm, was hired out to other plantation owners for that purpose, and was regarded as a valuable slave."[47] Lewis Jones said that his father, a breeding slave owned by a slaveholder named Fred Tate, was forced by his master to reproduce fifty slave-children by seven different bondswomen.[48]

Although the Texas ex-slave Elige Davison was married, his owner forbade him from having just one woman. A breeding slave as well, Davidson recalled that his master assigned him about fifteen slave-women and compelled him to father slave-children. He had no recollection of the precise number of children he fathered, but he knew they numbered over one hundred.[49]

We know that some slaveholders bred strong healthy slaves as one would breed animals, but the North Carolina ex-slave Cornelia Andrews told us that some sterilized sickly slaves because they considered them an economic risk. She stated, "Yo' knows dey ain't lat no little runty nigger have no chilluns. Naw sir, dey ain't, dey operate on dem lak dey does male hogs so's dat dey can't have no little runty chilluns."[50]

Assigning bondswomen sex mates and forcing them to bear slave-children against their will, whether for their owners or for the market, probably bore for many the same psychological consequences as rape. The master of Texas ex-slave Rose Williams forced her against her will to mate with a slave of his choosing. She never forgot the experience and vowed never to marry or have more children after she gained her freedom. What follows is her vivid recollection of the event:

Massa Black calls me to de block and de auction man say, "What am I offer for dis portly, strong wench. She's never been 'bused and will make a good breeder". . . . [T]he auction man say, "She am sold . . . to Mr. Hawkins". . . . Dere am one thing Massa Hawkins does to me what I can't shunt from my mind. . . . What he done am force me to live with dat . . . Rufus, 'gainst my wants. . . . I's about sixteen years old. . . . He am big . . . . I say to myse'f, "I's not gwine to live with dat Rufus." Dat night when him come in de cabin, I grabs the poker and sets on the bench and says, "Git from me . . . 'fore I busts you brains and stomp on them." Den nex' day de massa call me and tell me, "Woman, I's pay big money for you and I's done dat cause I wants you to raise me chillun. I's put you with Rufus for dat purpose. Now, if you doesn't want a whippin' at de stake, you do what I wants." I thinks 'bout Massa buyin' me offen de block and savin' me from bein' sep'rated from my folks, and 'bout bein' whipped at the stake. Der it am. What am I to do? I 'cides to do as de massa wish and so I yields. . . . I never marries, 'cause one 'sperience am 'nuf . . . . After what I does for de massa, I's never want no truck with any man. De Lawd forgive dis cullud woman, but he have to 'scuse me and look for some others for to 'plenish de earth.[51]

Bondswomen who were unwilling to comply with their owners' reproductive demands must have experienced humiliation and a loss of pride and self-esteem when they were sexually violated, but enslavement required the slave-labor force to reproduce itself. The advances in the manufacturing processes in England fueled her increasing demand for the South's cotton fiber, and the New England school teacher Eli Whitney facilitated the seeding of that cotton fiber through his 1793 invention and patent of the cotton gin. The demise of the Atlantic Slave Trade and the anticipated growth of the South's cotton industry compelled materialistic slaveholders to increase their domestic production of slaves.

By 1860, the slave population in the United States had increased to almost 4,000,000, making it possible for the Southern states to annually produce 5,387,000 bales of cotton.[52] The rapid growth of the South's cotton industry would not have been possible without the great abundance of cheap land located further southwest and the increasing supply of slave labor, the latter—in large part—the result of the slaveholders' practice of domestic slave breeding. Indeed, in 1858 an anonymous author of *The Profits of Farming* wrote, "I would not own any gang of Negroes where there was no increase."[53]

Notes

1. John Hope Franklin and Alfred A. Moss, Jr., *From Slavery to Freedom*, 6th ed. (New York: Alfred A. Knopf, Inc., 1988), 79.

2. The slave population in the United States increased from 1,191,362 in 1810 to 3,953,760 in 1860. *Statistics of the Population of the United States, Embracing the Tables of Race, Nationality, Sex, Selected Ages and Occupations . . . Compiled from the Original Returns of the Ninth Census (June 1, 1870)* (Wash., D.C.: U.S. Government Printing Office, 1872), 7.

3. Claud Anderson, Ed.D, *Black Labor, White Wealth: The Search for Power and Economic Justice* (Edgewood, Md.: Duncan & Duncan, Inc., 1994) 133; Franklin and Moss, *From Slavery to Freedom*, 118.

4. In the United States, the number of bondswomen to every 100 bondsmen between 1820 and 1860 ranged from 95.1 to 99.9. John W. Blassingame, *The Slave Community: Plantation Life in the Ante-Bellum South*, rev. ed. (Cary, North Carolina: Oxford University Press, 1979), 150.

5. Franklin and Moss, *From Slavery to Freedom*, 106.

6. For example, Kenneth M. Stampp wrote, "Evidence of systematic slave breeding is scarce, not only because it is unlikely that many engaged in it but because written records of such activities would be seldom kept." Kenneth M. Stampp, *The Peculiar Institution: Slavery in the Ante-Bellum South* (New York: Vintage Books, 1956), 245. Nonetheless, he insisted that if it did occur, it was not because white slaveholders forced their female slaves to have sex, but because masters gave them positive incentives. He wrote, "Seldom did female chattels disappoint their owner. After all, sexual promiscuity brought them rewards rather than penalties." "The slaveholder's intervention in the process of procreation," concluded Stampp, "was usually limited to provid-

ing slave women with favorable conditions and incentives." Stampp, *The Peculiar Institution*, 248, 251.

7. Franklin and Moss, *From Slavery to Freedom*, 106.

8. Fredrick Law Olmstead, *Journey and Explorations in the Cotton Kingdom*, vol. 1 (London: S. Low, Son & Co., 1861), 57-58.

9. James Oakes, *The Ruling Race: A History of American Slaveholders* (New York: Alfred A. Knopf, Inc., 1982), 74. Oakes took the quote from the Fitzpatrick Papers, August 20, 1849.

10. *Born in Slavery: Slave Narratives from the Federal Writers' Project, 1936-1938* (Wash., D.C.: Library of Congress, 2001), Georgia Narratives, vol. 4, part 2, 50. <memory.loc.gov/ammem/snhtml/snhome> (15 April 2006).

11. *Born in Slavery: Slave Narratives from the Federal Writers' Project*, Georgia Narratives, vol. 4, part 1, 191.

12. *Born in Slavery: Slave Narratives from the Federal Writers' Project*, Arkansas Narratives, vol. 2, part 1, 299.

13. Deborah Gray White, *Ar'n't I a Woman?: Female Slaves in the Plantation South* (New York: W. W. Norton & Co., 1985), 110.

14. Thomas D. Morris, *Southern Slavery and the Law 1619-1860* (Chapel Hill: University of North Carolina Press, 1996), 307.

15. White, *Ar'n't I a Woman*, 97-98.

16. Rebecca Latimer Felton, *Country Life in Georgia in the Days of My Youth: Electronic Edition* (Atlanta, Georgia: Index Printing Company, 1919), 79. <docsouth.unc.edu/felton> (12 Feb. 2006).

17. James Mellon, ed., *Bullwhip Days: The Slaves Remember* (New York: Avon Books, 1990), 147; George P. Rawick, ed., *The American Slave: A Composite Autobiography*, 41 vol. (Westport, Conn.: Greenwood Publishing Co., 1972), North Carolina, part 2, 434.

18. Norman Y. Yetman, ed., *Voices from Slavery: 100 Authentic Slave Narratives* (Toronto: General Publishing Company, Ltd., 2000), 228.

19. *Born in Slavery: Slave Narratives from the Federal Writers' Project*, Arkansas Narratives, vol. 2, part 1, 168.

20. *Born in Slavery: Slave Narratives from the Federal Writers' Project*, Georgia Narratives, vol. 4, part 2, 50.

21. William Goodell, *The American Slave Code in Theory and Practice: Its Distinctive Features Shown by Its Statutes, Judicial Decisions, and Illustrative Facts* (New York: American and Foreign Anti-Slavery Society, 1853), part 1, ch. 5, 84; Rev. Theodore D. Weld et al, ed., *Slavery as It Is: Testimony of a Thousand Witnesses* (New York: American Anti-Slavery Society, 1839), 175.

22. Felton, *Country Life in Georgia in the Days of My Youth*, 79.

23. White, *Ar'n't I a Woman?*, 90.

24. White, *Ar'n't I a Woman?*, 69.

25. *Born in Slavery: Slave Narratives from the Federal Writers' Project*, Arkansas Narratives, vol. 2, part 3, 339.

26. Yetman, *Voices from Slavery*, 164-165.

27. Susan Brownmiller, *Against Our Will* (New York; Bantam Books, 1975), 167.

28. John C. Perry, *Myths & Realities of American Slavery* (Shippensburg, Pa.: Burd Street Press, 2002), 139; White, *Ar'n't I a Woman?*, 98-99.

29. *Born in Slavery: Slave Narratives from the Federal Writers' Project*, Georgia Narratives, vol. 4, part 1, 191.

30. Yetman, *Voices from Slavery*, 39.

31. Rawick, *The American Slave*, Texas, part 3, 191.

32. *Born in Slavery: Slave Narratives from the Federal Writers' Project*, Arkansas Narratives, vol. 2, part 2, 132.

33. Yetman, *Voices from Slavery*, 288.

34. *Born in Slavery: Slave Narratives from the Federal Writers' Project*, Arkansas Narratives, vol. 2, part 7, 138.

35. Rawick, *The American Slave*, North Carolina, part 2, 78.

36. Rawick, *The American Slave*, North Carolina, part 2, 434.

37. William Wells Brown, *Narrative of William Wells Brown, A Fugitive Slave* (Boston: Published at Anti-slavery Office, No. 25 Cornhill, 1847), 89.

38. John Brown, *Slave Life in Georgia: Narrative of the Life, Sufferings and Escape of John Brown, A Fugitive Slave, Now in England* (London, 1855), 40.

39. Yetman, *Voices from Slavery*, 70.

40. *Born in Slavery: Slave Narratives from the Federal Writers' Project*, Arkansas Narratives, vol. 2, part 7, 139.

41. Yetman, *Voices from Slavery*, 277; *Born in Slavery: Slave Narratives from the Federal Writers' Project*, North Carolina Narratives, vol. 11, part 2, 434.

42. *Born in Slavery: Slave Narratives from the Federal Writers' Project*, Florida Narratives, vol. 3, 167.

43. *Born in Slavery: Slave Narratives from the Federal Writers' Project*, Florida Narratives, vol. 3, 127.

44. *Born in Slavery: Slave Narratives from the Federal Writers' Project*, Florida Narratives, vol. 3, 128.

45. *Born in Slavery: Slave Narratives from the Federal Writers' Project*, Texas Narratives, vol. 16, part 4, 189.

46. *Born in Slavery: Slave Narratives from the Federal Writers' Project*, Arkansas Narratives, vol. 2, part 4, 174.

47. *Born in Slavery: Slave Narratives from the Federal Writers' Project*, Indiana Narratives, vol. 5, 186.

48. Mellon, *Bullwhip Days*, 149.

49. Yetman, *Voices from Slavery*, 92.

50. Rawick, *The American Slave*, North Carolina, part 1, 31.

51. Mellon, *Bullwhip Days*, 128-32.

52. Franklin and Moss, *From Slavery to Freedom*, 114.

53. Herbert G. Gutman, *The Black Family in Slavery and Freedom 1750-1925* (New York: Vintage Books, 1977), 77.

CHAPTER THIRTEEN

Begetting Children for Profit

Most American historians have not examined the slaveholder's economic rationale for white-on-black rape, either because they mischaracterize it solely as an act of passion or adventure, or they deny its widespread occurrence. Kenneth Stampp, for example, described the rapes of bondswomen by white adolescents as "casual adventures in sexual experimentation." In his mind, white college students and other white men who raped slave-women were "demanding favors."[1] John Perry denied that widespread master-on-slave rape occurred during the ante-bellum period and asked, "Would a slaveowner risk at least consternation of his slaves and more likely the discipline problem his philandering would cause?"[2] Henry Bibb answered his question in the affirmative, charging that slaveholders "can and do enter at night or day the lodging places of the slaves; break up bonds of affectionate families, [and] destroy all their domestic and social union for life." Bibb noted that they were able to do so because the laws of the South afforded slaves no protection.[3] Asked whether or not white men respected as married women the wives of slaves, a Petersburg, Virginia slave replied, "No mass'r dey don't make no diff'rence wedder de colored women is married or not. White folks jest do what dey have a mind to wid dem."[4]

Black bondswomen who were beautiful were most likely to be raped by white men. In fact, Linda Brent observed that if God bestowed beauty on the bondswoman, it would prove her greatest curse. "That which commands admiration in the white woman," wrote Brent, "only hastens the degradation of the female slave."[5] Louisa "Nor" Everett agreed, saying that quite often her master and even his guests would have sex with his female slaves, "choosing for themselves the prettiest of the young women." She said, "Sometimes they forced the unhappy husbands and lovers of their victims to look on."[6] Richard Macks also informed us that he knew of several cases in which "good-looking" slave-women paid the price for their beauty as victims of rape, but he found those cases too distasteful to discuss.[7]

Leslie Howard Owens believed that master-on-slave rape probably intensified animosities between the races and may have caused disunity within the slave family.[8] In and of itself, that potentially could have created a slave discipline problem for the slaveholder. But an advantage—chiefly economic—outweighed any potential control problem the master's act of sexual assault may have caused. As the demand for slave labor increased, the materialistically obsessed slaveholder attempted to increase the whole population of his most valuable asset—his slaves; but he wanted to increase each slave's individual market value as well. The slaveholder understood that forcibly impregnating bondswomen through the use of potent white men served a duel purpose: it increased his slave labor supply and it produced an "improved" mixed breed of mulatto slaves—slaves who commanded a higher price on the auction block.

Laws throughout the ante-bellum South prohibited whites from marrying blacks—slaves or free—as such marriages would have undermined the American slavery regime. Marriage laws in North Carolina and South Carolina, for example, forbade and criminalized white-black marriages. No similar law, however, prohibited whites from having sex with black slaves in the Southern states.[9] Far from representing a threat to the American slavery regime, interracial sex, argued A. Leon Higginbotham Jr., "served as its life blood."[10] It mattered not that the child born of interracial sex had part "white" blood. As early as 1662, the colony of Virginia enacted a law requiring all children born in that colony to be held bond or free according to the status of their mother.[11] Maryland passed a similar law in 1681.[12]

The laws of the ante-bellum South considered a mere drop of African blood sufficient to pollute an ocean of European blood, consigning that mixed-blood child to a lifetime of servitude because his mother was a slave. The Arkansas ex-slave Rachel Fairley's aunt bore two mulatto slave-children fathered by her master. Fairley said, "They were as white as the white children nearly but their mother was a colored women. That made the difference."[13]

Fully backed by the legal system, the slaveholder insisted that raping his slave-woman was his property right, and one economic privilege or benefit of that right was begetting mulatto children from the act and placing them on the slave auction block for his material gain. Not a few slaveowners wanted to reproduce more profitable young mulatto slave-children, and as one traveler journeying across the South observed, "The master's licentiousness" did "breed for him a peculiarly valuable stock of cattle."[14]

The ideology of white supremacy underpinned the American slavery regime; consequently, in the matter of color the slaveholding class de-valued blackness and assigned a relatively higher market value to whiteness. In 1850, one traveler thus wrote, "Great solicitude is often manifested that breeding wenches, as they call them, should be the mothers of mulatto children, as nearer the young slaves approach to white the higher the price will be, especially if they are females."[15]

The slaveholder's demand for more valuable mulatto slaves was the major impetus behind his impregnation of the bondswoman. Touring New Orleans between 1829 and 1830, the English traveler Simon Ansley Ferrall noted, "If the offspring, a mulatto, be a handsome female, from $800 to $1,000 may be obtained for her in the Orleans market."[16] John Perry insists that there was a severe social stigma attached to interracial sexual activities in the nineteenth century.[17] While the white slaveholding class may have officially condemned interracial sex because there may have been a social stigma associated with it, it was hardly severe enough to dissuade slaveholders from raping their bondswomen for gain.

During the ante-bellum period, observers from not only the South and the North, but from abroad as well, could not help but comment on what they perceived as the South's growing mulatto slave population. Writing in 1836, the traveler Fredrick Marryat referred to a system of amalgamation which had "been carried to such an extent that you very often meet with slaves whose skins are whiter than their master's!"[18] Georgian Rebecca L. Felton recalled "violations of the moral law that made mulattoes as common as blackberries."[19] The Northern observer Mrs. A. M. French opined that it was slavery alone that made the South "the African bleaching ground."[20]

While some white mistresses bitterly acknowledged the fact of their husbands' interracial sexual activities, others coped with those activities by sticking their proverbial heads in the sand; they were in denial. The South Carolina ex-slave Mom Ryer Emmanuel, for example, said that her mistress was very proud of all the black slave-children playing around on her front steps, but she found the only "yellow" one in the group troubling. The mistress asked that child, "Who's your papa?" Too young to know better, the slave-child told his owner exactly what his mother had told him. According to Mom Ryer Emmanuel, the mistress replied, "Well, get off my step. Get off and stay off there 'cause you don't noways belong to me."[21]

In 1861, Mary Boykin Chesnut remarked on all the mulatto slave-children she saw while living on a Camden, South Carolina plantation. She wrote:

Old men live all in one house with their wives and their concubines; and the mulattoes one sees in every family partly resemble the white children. Any lady is ready to tell you who is the father of all the mulatto children in everybody's household but her own. Those she seems to think, drop from the clouds.[22]

In the federally-funded WPA interviews conducted during the 1930s, several former slaves talked openly about the masters' practice of impregnating their bondswomen for profit. One even had a name for slaveholders who fathered mulatto children. Martha Allen referred to her mulatto father's master—her grandfather—as a "Carpet Gitter."[23] But how widespread was the practice? From the testimony of several ex-slaves from North Carolina, it appears that it was commonplace. For example, the former slave Reverend

Squire Dowd said that bondswomen having children by the master was common. His relatives on his mother's side of the family were mixed-blooded.[24] Lizzie Williams also told us that many black women bore "chillen for de massa, dat is if de massa [was] a mean man." She said that the slaveholders just told the bondswomen "what to do and dey [knew] better dan to fuss."[25] Cognizant of many bondswomen bearing children of white slaveowners, W. L. Post similarly stated, "She know better than to not do what they say." Post recalled that the masters would take those very same children—their own flesh and blood—and would make slaves out of them.[26]

From the testimony of former slaves from other Southern states, it also is apparent that master-on-slave rape for profit was prevalent. Born in 1843, the Georgia ex-slave Jack Maddox recalled that white slaveholders fathered plenty children of black women. He said, "They didn't ask them. They just took them."[27] Carrie Mason, another former slave from Georgia, said that slave impregnation by the master or his sons "happened a lot in them days." She remembered one slaveholder who would tell his sons to go down to the slave quarters and reproduce more mulatto slave-children.[28] The Texas ex-slave Chris Franklin also remembered "lots of places where de young massas has heirs" by black women.[29] Charlotte Martin similarly informed us that her owner sometimes had sexual relations with his bondswomen because the products of miscegenation were very remunerative. She said that the mulatto offspring were in great demand as house servants.[30] The Mississippi-born ex-slave Salomon Oliver commented on his master John A. Miller's interracial sexual activities. He said, "Master John was bad after the slave-women. A yellow child showed up every once in a while." Oliver exclaimed, "My own Mammy, Mary, was the master's own daughter!"[31]

Former slaves from Oklahoma gave us similar accounts. John White told us, "Sometimes the white folks go around the slave quarters for the night. . . . The slaves talked about it amongst themselves. After a while they'd be a new baby. Yellow."[32] George G. King recalled that two of his older sisters, Eva and Laura, were fathered by a white man.[33] Harriet Robinson, when interviewed as a ninety-five-year-old former slave from Oklahoma, said that her sister Liza— herself a mulatto slave—bore three children of her master's son.[34]

Slaveholders compelled other bondswomen by the threat of death or bodily harm to submit to impregnation by non-slaveholding whites. The historian Arthur W. Calhoun in fact noted "the tradition of the importation of college boys from the North to spend a profitable summer improving the slave breed."[35] Because white college students from the North were taught that they were dealing with an inferior race, they could be persuaded that raping black bondswomen was a lucrative summer job. Indeed, slaveholders gave financial rewards to white men who fathered mulatto slaves.[36] One actually offered a white man twenty dollars for every impregnation of a slave-woman to "improve the breed."[37]

Mixed-Blood Slave-Children for Sale

It is a myth that large numbers of slaveholders gave protection to their mixed-blood slave-children and generally emancipated them. Although there were a disproportionate number of mulattoes in the free black population, seldom did slaveholders free their mulatto children.[38] Many suffered greatly in bondage, as their fathers or their white siblings sold them to slave traders. In 1836, the foreign observer Fredrick Marryat noted one congressman, a Georgian, who brought into the world a family of mulatto slave-children, only to sell them all by public auction during his lifetime.[39] Touring the South between the years 1829 and 1830, Simon Ansley Ferrall found it "an occurrence of no uncommon nature to see the Christian father sell his own daughter" or "the brother his own sister, by the same father."[40] A former slave from Louisiana, Martha Johnson, provided the example of her mulatto slave-mother; she was sold by her master's son—her half-brother—after her father died.[41]

Several former slaves recalled that if the price was right, slaveholders would sell their mulatto slave-children just like other slaves.[42] The South Carolina ex-slave Savilla Burrell, for example, said that her master sold all his mulatto children from their mother to a slave trader.[43] Isiah Green told us that his mulatto grandmother, Betsy Willis, was placed on the auction block by her slaveholding father.[44] Mollie Kinsey also remembered many young mulatto slave-girls who were sold by their fathers—taken right out of the yards with their white children and "sold like herds of cattle."[45]

Although mulatto bondswomen were in great demand as house servants, the foreign traveler Francis William Newman observed that the beautiful mulatto slave-girls—some even reared in their slaveholding fathers' houses—were sold after their fathers died, or because of financial difficulties, to white men for their sexual gratification.[46] Slave traders shackled large numbers of young mulatto bondswomen, transported them to Southern cities, and sold them at enormous prices to white men. Asked the price of a "mixed-blood" on sale at Alexandria, Virginia, one slave trader replied, "We can't afford to sell the girl Emily for less than $1,800. We have two or three offers for Emily from gentlemen from the South."[47]

Generally, slaveholders did not acknowledge their mulatto slave-children. The white supremicist political activist Rebecca L. Felton in fact noted, "The crime that made slavery a curse lies in the fact that unbridled lust placed the children of bad white men in slave pens, on auction blocks, and no regard was shown to parentage or parental responsibility in such matters."[48] Lizzie Williams recalled a mulatto slave-child named Emily whose slaveholding father paid no more attention to her than to the rest of his slaves.[49] The ex-slave Annie L. Burton's mistress often told her that her father was a slaveholder who owned a plantation a few miles from the one on which she resided. Burton noted that she never spoke to her father and could not remember that he ever noticed her or in any way acknowledged her as his child.[50] Apparently, he considered her as just another slave-child. At least, Burton knew her father's identity and where he lived. John Thomas Williams, a less fortunate North Carolina-born mulatto ex-slave, did not know his father, his mother, or any of his relatives. He said,

> I have asked thousands of questions trying to find out who my people are but no one has ever told me who I am or who my people are. If I have any brothers and sisters, I don't know it. I have nothing to say about being partly white. I leave that to your imagination.[51]

In 1836, Harriet Martineau commented on the insightful observation of a Southern planter concerning slaveholders who father and sell mulatto children. She wrote,

> A gentleman of the highest character, a Southern planter, observed that the very general connection of white gentlemen with their female slaves introduced a mulatto race whose numbers would become dangerous if . . . their white parents were permitted to render them free. The liberty of emancipating them was therefore abolished, while the selling of them remained. . . . These planters, who sell their offspring for the sake of their purses, dare to raise the cry of "amalgamation" against the abolitionists of the North.[52]

Some masters sold not only their mulatto slave-children, but they sold the children's mothers as well. For instance, the slaveholder John Street fathered the Kentucky ex-slave Amy Elizabeth Patterson—the first-born child of her slave-mother. Amy Elizabeth said that her owner operated a slave agency where he collected slaves and annually sold them to dealers in human flesh. Contemplating a move to another territory, Street decided to auction off his entire inventory of slaves, including his daughter Amy Elizabeth and her mother, to the highest bidder. Clearly humiliated when her father had placed her on the auction block, Amy Elizabeth Patterson said,

> That was the greatest crime ever visited on the United States. It was worse than the cruelty of overseers, worse than hunger . . . but when a father can sell his own child—humiliate his own daughter by auctioning her on the slave block—what good could be expected where such practices were allowed? . . . Yes, slavery is a curse to this nation, a curse which still shows itself in hundreds of homes where mulatto faces are evidence of a heinous sin, and proof that there has been a time when American fathers sold their children at the slave marts of America.[53]

Linda Brent observed that the mistresses did not trouble themselves either about selling their husbands' mulatto children because they regarded those "children as property, as marketable as pigs on the plantation." She noted that it was seldom that they did not make them aware of the fact that they were property "by passing them into the slave trader's hands as soon as possible."[54]

Indeed, some slaveholding husbands sold light-complexioned slave-children at the behest of their embarrassed or bitter wives. Douglas Dorsey, a former slave from Florida, explained to his interviewer why his mistress asked that his light-skinned brother be sold. The interviewer, James Johnson, wrote the following:

> To his mother and father was born a little baby boy, whose complexion was rather light. Mrs. Matair at once began accusing Colonel Matair [of] being the father of the child. Naturally the colonel denied [it], but Mrs. Matair kept harassing him about it until he finally agreed to his wife's desire and sold the child. It was taken from its mother's breast at the age of eight months and auctioned off on the first day of January to the highest bidder.[55]

Consider the emotional and psychological devastation suffered by that slave-mother when her master snatched her newborn from her breast and sold the baby to a slave trader. Unburdened by conscience, slaveholders believed that it was perfectly natural to sell their own flesh and blood—to beget children for profit.[56]

Since it was common for slaveholders to father mulatto children and sell them for gain, we might wonder whether or not respect for the slave family took a back seat to the master's economic interests. What have American historians said about the slaveholder's decision to break up black slave families? Over the last forty years, why have they insisted that masters generally took into account a moral consideration and an economic consideration in deciding to sell their slaves from their loved ones when, in fact, they typically took into account only an economic one? In Part Three, we will consider what American historians have written and ex-slaves have told us about the break-up of slave families, and we will explore that inhumane facet of ante-bellum-era American slavery.

Notes

1. Kenneth Stampp noted that "most of the relationships between slave-women and males of the slaveholding class were the casual adventures of adolescents engaged in sexual experimentation, of college students and of older bachelors or widows periodically demanding favors of one of their female chattels." Kenneth M. Stampp, *The Peculiar Institution: Slavery in the Ante-Bellum South* (New York: Vintage Books, 1956), 355.

2. John C. Perry, *Myths & Realities of American Slavery* (Shippensburg, Pa.: Burd Street Press, 2002), 127.

3. Gilbert Osofsky, ed., *Puttin' On Ole Massa* (New York: Harper & Row Publishers, 1969), 77.

4. James Redpath, *The Roving Editor: or, Talks With Slaves in the Southern States* (New York: A.B. Burdick Publisher, 1859), 93.

5. Harriett Brent Jacobs, *Incidents in the Life of a Slave Girl*, ed. L. Maria Child (Boston: Act of Congress, 1861), 46.

6. *Born in Slavery: Slave Narratives from the Federal Writers' Project, 1936-1938* (Wash., D.C.: Library of Congress, 2001), Florida Narratives, vol. 3, 127 <memory.loc.gov/ammem/snhtml/snhome> (15 April 2006).

7. *Born in Slavery: Slave Narratives from the Federal Writers' Project*, Maryland Narratives, vol. 8, 53.

8. Leslie Howard Owens, *This Species of Property* (New York: Oxford University Press, Inc., 1976), 212.

9. Claud Anderson, Ed.D., *Black Labor, White Wealth: The Search for Power and Economic Justice* (Edgewood, Md.: Duncan & Duncan, Inc., 1994), 223.

10. A. Leon Higginbotham, Jr., *Shades of Freedom: Racial Politics and Presumptions of the American Legal Process* (New York: Oxford University Press, 1996), 44.

11. John Hope Franklin and Alfred A. Moss, Jr., *From Slavery to Freedom*, 6th ed. (New York: Alfred A. Knopf, Inc., 1988), 54.

12. Franklin and Moss, *From Slavery to Freedom*, 55.

13. *Born in Slavery: Slave Narratives from the Federal Writers' Project*, Arkansas Narratives, vol. 2, part 2, 261.

14. Francis William Newman, *Character of the Southern States* (Manchester, England: Union and Emancipation Depot, 1863), 7.

15. Reverend Charles Elliott, D.D., Rev. B. F. Tefft, D.D., eds., *Sinfulness of American Slavery*, vol. 1 (L. Swormstedt and J. H. Power, 1850), 154.

16. Simon Ansley Ferrall, *A Ramble of Six Thousand Miles Through the United States of America* (London: E. Wilson, Publisher, 1832), 195.

17. Perry, *Myths & Realities of American Slavery*, 127.

18. Fredrick Marryat, *A Diary in America* (1836; reprint New York: Alfred A. Knopf, 1962), 280.

19. Rebecca Latimer Felton, *Country Life in Georgia in the Days of My Youth: Electronic Edition* (Atlanta, Ga.: Index Printing Company, 1919), 79. <docsouth.unc.edu/felton> (12 Feb. 2006).

20. Mrs. A. M. French, *Slavery in South Carolina and the Ex-slaves; or, The Port Royal Mission* (New York: Winchell M. French, 1862), 139.

21. *Born in Slavery: Slave Narratives from the Federal Writers' Project*, South Carolina Narratives, vol. 14, part 2, 14.

22. Mary Boykin Chesnut, *A Diary from Dixie* (Boston: Houghton Mifflin Co., 1949), 21.

23. *Born in Slavery: Slave Narratives from the Federal Writers' Project*, North Carolina Narratives, vol. 11, part 1, 14.

24. *Born in Slavery: Slave Narratives from the Federal Writers' Project*, North Carolina Narratives, vol. 11, part 1, 267.

25. Norman Y. Yetman, ed., *Voices from Slavery: 100 Authentic Slave Narratives* (Toronto: General Publishing company, Ltd., 2000), 317.

26. Yetman, *Voices from Slavery*, 37.

27. James Mellon, ed., *Bullwhip Days: The Slaves Remember* (New York: Avon Books, 1990), 121.

28. Andrew Waters, ed., *On Jordan's Stormy Banks* (Winston-Salem, N.C.: John F. Blair, Publisher, 2000), 140.

29. *Born in Slavery: Slave Narratives from the Federal Writers' Project*, Texas Narratives, vol. 16, part 2, 57.

30. *Born in Slavery: Slave Narratives from the Federal Writers' Project*, Florida Narratives, vol. 3, 167.

31. *Born in Slavery: Slave Narratives from the Federal Writers' Project*, Oklahoma Narratives, vol. 13, 233.

32. *Born in Slavery: Slave Narratives from the Federal Writers' Project*, Oklahoma Narratives, vol. 13, 325.

33. *Born in Slavery: Slave Narratives from the Federal Writers' Project*, Oklahoma Narratives, vol. 13, 167.

34. *Born in Slavery: Slave Narratives from the Federal Writers' Project*, Oklahoma Narratives, vol. 13, 273.

35. Arthur W. Calhoun, *A Social History of the American Family from Colonial Times to the Present*, vol. 2 (Cleveland: The Arthur H. Clark Co., 1917), 246.

36. Reverend Charles Elliott, D.D., Rev. B. F. Tefft, D.D., eds., *Sinfulness of American Slavery*, vol. 1 (L. Swormstedt and J. H. Power, 1850), 154.

37. Calhoun, *A Social History of the American Family*, 245.

38. E. Franklin Frazier noted, "In 1850, an estimated 37% of the free Negro population in the United States," and "probably little more than 10% of the slave population had white ancestry." E. Franklin Frazier, *Black Bourgeoisie* (New York: Collier Books, 1962), 116.

39. Marryat, *A Diary in America*, 281.

40. Simon Ansley Ferrall, *A Ramble of Six Thousand Miles Through the United States of America* (London: E. Wilson, Publisher, 1832), 195.

41. *Born in Slavery: Slave Narratives from the Federal Writers' Project*, Arkansas Narratives, vol. 2, part 4, 122.

42. *Born in Slavery: Slave Narratives from the Federal Writers' Project*, Texas Narratives, vol. 16, part 2, 57; Georgia Narratives, vol. 4, part 1, 44; Oklahoma Narratives, vol. 13, 325.

43. George P. Rawick, ed., *The American Slave: A Composite Autobiography*, 41 vols. (Westport, Conn.: Greenwood Publishing Co., 1972), South Carolina, part 1, 150.

44. *Born in Slavery: Slave Narratives from the Federal Writers' Project*, Georgia Narratives, vol. 4, part 2, 50.

45. Waters, *On Jordan's Stormy Banks*, 20.

46. Newman, *Character of the Southern States*, 7.

47. Calhoun, *A Social History of the American Family*, 298.

48. Felton, *Country Life in Georgia in the Days of My Youth*, 93.

49. Yetman, *Voices from Slavery*, 317.

50. Annie L. Burton, *Memories of Childhood's Slavery Days* (Boston: Ross Publishing Co., 1909), 49-51.

51. *Born in Slavery: Slave Narratives from the Federal Writers' Project*, North Carolina Narratives, vol. 11, part 2, 391-92.

52. Harriet Martineau, *Society in America*, vol. 3 (London: Saunders & Otley, 1837), 328-29.

53. *Born in Slavery: Slave Narratives from the Federal Writers' Project*, Indiana Narratives, vol. 5, 150-52.

54. Jacobs, *Incidents in the Life of a Slave Girl*, 57.

55. *Born in Slavery: Slave Narratives from the Federal Writers' Project*, Florida Narratives, vol. 3, 95.

56. Calhoun, *A Social History of the American Family*, 301.

PART THREE

Slave Family Break-Ups

CHAPTER FOURTEEN

The Humane Home-Breaker in Slavery Historiography

In Africa, the stability of the black family periodically might have been disturbed by a calamity of nature; but in the ante-bellum South, the stability of that family was in constant jeopardy. The slaveholder decided the slave family's fate. First and foremost, the slaves had to satisfy the economic needs of their owners, and their existence as a family unit was precarious because the slave family's survival was dependent on those needs. Whether one was the mother or the father, the head of that family understood this. Many slaves feared the threat of sale for good reason. Slaveowners might approve of a family and might even have promised not to separate it, but most would have broken that promise at any time if there were a change in financial plans. The slaveholder's respect, if any, for the black slave family took a back seat to his pecuniary interest.

Much of American slavery historiography expresses the fallacy that the typical slaveholder lived a contradictory double role of patriarch and estate manager. One view among historians was that the slaveholder took into account two separate considerations when breaking up a slave family: a moral one and an economic one. This view depicts a perplexed master, experiencing a *crise de conscience*—a slaveholder suffering psychic agony and torment caused by two constantly warring considerations. Some American slavery historians argue that because the master's role as a patriarch left him morally concerned about the stability of his slave families, breaking them up would have been his option of last resort. In the following passage, for example, Kenneth Stampp depicts slaveholders who exercised the option to sell their slaves only under the most financially calamitous circumstances:

The more conscientious slaveholders made great financial sacrifices to avoid dealing with "speculators." Some patriarchal masters in Virginia and elsewhere lived on the edge of bankruptcy rather than seeking solvency through sale of all or part of their "people." Other masters, more concerned about social prestige, feared to lose rank by marketing bondsmen. When necessity dictated sales, masters often gave convincing evidence of the distress this misfortune caused them . . . . The majority of slaveholders agreed that only the most calamitous circumstances could justify dealings with professional traders . . . . Perhaps only a few masters wished to regard slaves as marketable commodities . . . .[1]

Among other historians, Stampp maintained that the slaveholder, responsive to public opinion and his own moral conscience, tried to convince his community of the appropriateness of selling his slave by persuading the community that the slave was disobedient.[2] In Stampp's view, the master's rationalization might have "protected him from loss of public esteem, but it did not always satisfy his troubled conscience."[3] The notion that a troubled conscience burdened the slaveholder is conjecture, though it is certainly true that the master's public relations strategy was to project the appearance of being humane. But concrete evidence that slaveholders typically sold slaves away from their loved ones for material gain belies the claim that their consciences were troubled. In fact, Stampp found that most slaveholders adopted an extremely broad definition of economic necessity, and that "[s]omehow their necessities kept the auctioneers busy and enabled the traders to conduct a thick traffic in human flesh."[4]

Leslie Howard Owens also depicted slaveholders who mulled over moral and economic considerations before selling their slaves. Noting legislative proposals in North Carolina which requested that the parental relation be acknowledged and protected by law and that the separation of slave-parents from their young children be forbidden under heavy pain and penalties, Owens wrote, "Though such memorials were frequent, legislators never heeded them, for their implementation would merely have served to increase the moral questions that bothered many slaveholders."[5] Despite offering little support for his claim, Owens argued that slaveholders typically showed concern when reaching the decision to split up a black slave family because the practice ran counter to what they felt to be right. Nonetheless, he acknowledged that the odds against survival of the slave family were formidable.[6]

Eugene Genovese contended as well that selling slaves from their families did not rest easy on the master's conscience. He wrote,

Many slaveholders went to impressive lengths to keep families together even at the price of considerable pecuniary loss, although as Kenneth Stampp forcefully insists, the great majority of slaveholders chose business over sentiment and broke up families when under financial pressure. But the choice did not rest easy on their conscience.[7]

Genovese is unable to accept that in considering the sale of a slave, generally speaking, expectation of profit or loss was the master's sole criterion. He insisted that the slaveholder operated within both an economic sphere and a moral sphere, and in the face of market pressure, he felt guilty about his inability to live up to his own paternalistic justification for slavery. "Masters," Genovese argued, "could not afford to be wholly indifferent to slave sensibilities." For the most part, however, they were wholly indifferent. A former slave from Virginia, Henry H. Butler, recalled that slaveholders expressed no compassion when a slave sale or trade was at hand. He saw the separation of husbands from wives, the separation of children from mothers, and the extreme grief of those from whom family members were snatched and sold away. Butler also observed slaveowners bullwhipping those grieving slaves for neglecting their work.[8] Perhaps Eugene Genovese claimed that masters experienced great conflict and torment when selling their slaves because he believed the paternalism propaganda. He wrote,

> No other issues so clearly exposed the hybrid nature of the regime; so clearly pitted economic interests against paternalism and defined limits beyond which the one could not reinforce the other. The problem and the contradiction it called forth therefore remained—*and so did the agony.*[9]

Like his contemporaries, Genovese did not question that slaveholders experienced agony and torment when separating slave family members. Yet, faced with solid evidence, he conceded—as did his contemporaries—that many masters did not respect their slave families' feelings and did not hesitate to sell slaves individually.[10]

Separation of slave family members through sale was an integral part of the American slavery regime; it was resorted to by heartless masters and those whom the white community might have perceived as more humane.[11] Writing over seventy-five years ago, Frederic Bancroft noted that even slaveholders of high standing who needed money sold their best slaves because they brought the most. "It was the money," wrote Bancroft, "not the purchasers or the slaves that mattered."[12] In the following passage, he explains that the master, concerned with merely projecting the appearance of being humane, applied expectation of profit or loss as his criterion in deciding to sell his slave:

> Virtually everybody preferred to be humane, according to Southern standards, when it was not financially disadvantageous or inconvenient to do so. Persons whose interest led them to be otherwise naturally wished to conceal the fact or tried to place blame elsewhere, for there was no respectability without *at least the appearance of being humane.* But slavery maintained as a profitable and convenient institution was essentially ruthless in general and inhumane in some of its main features . . . . Thus not humanity but expectation of profit or loss was the criterion.[13]

Since the stability of the slave family unit was precarious—dependent on the slaveholder's economic needs, were strong emotional bonds allowed to develop among immediate slave family members? In the next chapter, we will examine the importance of the slave family and determine what role, if any, it played in helping the slave to cope with daily living conditions under the American slavery regime.

Notes

1. Kenneth M. Stampp, *The Peculiar Institution: Slavery in the Ante-Bellum South* (New York: Vintage Books, 1956), 239-40.

2. See, Peter J. Parish, *Slavery: History and Historians* (New York: Harper & Row Publishers, 1989), 1-9.

3. Stampp, *The Peculiar Institution*, 242.

4. Stampp, *The Peculiar Institution*, 242.

5. Leslie Howard Owens, *This Species of Property* (New York: Oxford University Press, Inc., 1976), 192.

6. Owens, *This Species of Property*, 183.

7. Eugene D. Genovese, *Roll, Jordan, Roll: The World the Slaves Made* (New York: Vintage Books, 1972), 453.

8. *Born in Slavery: Slave Narratives from the Federal Writers' Project, 1936-1938,* Texas Narratives, vol. 16, part 1, p. 180 (Wash., D.C.: Library of Congress, 2001) <memory.loc.gov/ammem/snhtml/snhome.html> (10 Feb. 2007).

9. Genovese, *Roll, Jordan, Roll*, 53. (emphasis mine)

10. Genovese, *Roll, Jordan, Roll*, 457.

11. Stanley Feldstein, *Once a Slave* (New York: William Morrow Company, Inc., 1971), 56.

12. Frederic Bancroft, *Slave Trading in the Old South* (Baltimore, Md.: J. H. Furst Company, 1931; reprinted New York: Fredrick Unger Publishing Company, 1959), 27.

13. Bancroft, *Slave Trading in the Old South*, 197-98. (emphasis mine)

CHAPTER FIFTEEN

The Importance of the Slave Family

The slave family unit was the slave's most important survival mechanism for two reasons: it served his emotional needs and it served his material needs—needs not served by his master. Nathan Irvin Huggins wrote about the atomizing features of slavery. He explained that the forces of the American slavery regime isolated the slave, separated him from his loved ones during the incessant toil of each day, and tried to relegate him to the status of a mere unit of cheap field labor.[1] But the compassion, respect, sympathetic understanding of the slave's suffering, and the love that the slave family offered served as buffers against the brutal reality of life under the slavery regime.

The slaves built strong family ties. They also strove to maintain family stability, allowing their family members to attend to their emotional needs. In no type of American autobiographies is more emphasis placed on the importance of a stable family than in the autobiographies of former slaves. From his own painful experience, the former slave Thomas H. Jones wrote about "the deep and fond affection which the slave cherishes in his heart for [his] home and [his] dear ones." Jones had no other tie to link him to "human family" but his "fervent love" for those who were with him "in relations of sympathy and devotion, in wrongs and wretchedness."[2] Commenting on the love his slave family gave him, the Indiana ex-slave Dr. George Washington Buckner said that although his family members were not properly housed, nourished, or clothed, they loved each other, loved their cabin homes, and were unhappy when compelled to part.[3]

David Brion Davis provides evidence of the slaves' strong family ties:

> The strength of family bonds is suggested by the thousands of slaves who ran away from their owners in search of family members separated through sale. The notion that blacks had weak family attachments is also countered by the swarms of freedmen who roamed the South at the end of the Civil War in search of their spouses, parents, or children and by the eager desire of freed people to legalize their marriages.[4]

Adult slave family members worked together, contributing meaningful labor and providing essential material resources for their families. Deborah Gray White correctly concluded that slave families were usually egalitarian and that "procuring extra provisions for the family was the shared responsibility of bondswoman and bondsman."[5]

Although some slaves were well fed by their owners, most were poorly nourished. The master's customary weekly allotment of food for each slave consisted of a peck to a peck and a half of corn, ground into meal for corn bread, and two-to-four pounds of bacon. Some slaves received a gallon of molasses as well.[6] The slaves prepared their own food. The typical slave in the ante-bellum South did not starve to death because long-term hunger would have diminished his productivity. As a general rule, however, his owner gave him inadequate food. The anti-slavery orator Frederick Douglass noted that the four slaves his master owned were allowed less than half of a bushel of corn meal per week and "very little else in the shape of meat or vegetables."[7] Louis Hughes, a former slave, comments on the masters' inability to understand that their slaves were undernourished:

> The idea never seemed to occur to the slaveholders that their slaves were getting no wages for their work and therefore, had nothing with which to procure what at times was necessary for their health and strength—palatable and nourishing food.[8]

In the United States—unlike in much of the Caribbean—more often than not, slaveholders did not allow their slaves to grow their own food, but those slaves whom their owners allowed to grow their own food depended on one another in familial arrangements, laboring together to supplement and vary their families' meager diets with vegetables. Charles Ball wrote about the gardens and patches that the slaves cultivated on Sunday, a day which the majority of slaves had off.[9] Other slave families looked after small garden patches on moon-lit nights and Saturday evenings.[10] The master of the Georgia ex-slave Dosia Harris allowed her family to have a little garden patch. She recalled that she would go to the family garden in the winter, cut down collard greens after the frost hit, take them to the cabin, and boil them for her family's dinner.[11]

Intent on keeping their slaves totally dependent, other slaveholders prohibited their slaves from profiting from the fruit of labor performed during their time off. For example, although Celestia Avery's master did not give his slaves much of a variety of food and permitted each slave family to raise its own vegetables, Avery told us that her master always required half of all the vegetables raised by each slave and that it was not permissible for a slave to sell any.[12] Similarly, according to the Georgia ex-slave George Eason, the produce from the garden that his owner allowed the slaves to cultivate could be used for home consumption only; under no circumstances could any of it be sold.[13]

Though this was generally not permissible, some slaves would steal away from the plantation at night and would hunt to provide meat for their families. The male slave's role as hunter and family provider helped him to develop an identity separate and apart from that assigned to him by his master. Josh Horn, an ex-slave from Alabama, remembered, "I's killed in the woods, 'cause us raised chillun fast, and us had a heap of 'em, sixteen, if I's members right, and soon's I found out dat I could help feed 'em dat way, I done a heap of hunting."[14] Former slaves from Georgia, John F. Van Hook and Georgia Baker, recalled that the slaves hunted rabbits, squirrels, raccoons, all kinds of birds, and were especially fond of hunting wild turkeys.[15] The ex-slave Callie Elder's grandfather hunted opossum at night, bringing back two or three at a time. He went fishing as well to supplement the family diet, catching minnow and other fish.[16]

Bondswomen also hunted to help supplement the family diet. "My mamma could hunt as good as any man," boasted Betty Brown, a former slave from Arkansas. Her mother traded various animal hides with peddlers for calico prints.[17] When the South Carolina ex-slave Sylvia Cannon's family became desperate for meat and could find nothing else, she made "death traps" with lids, baited them with cabbage and corn, and caught rabbits and birds.[18]

As a general rule, slaveholders provided barely adequate clothing for all but privileged house slaves who made up a small minority of the slave population. The ninety-one-year-old Louisiana ex-slave Louis Love saw very young slave-children wearing no pants.[19] Henry Johnson said that he never knew what a shirt was until he was over twenty years of age.[20] Other slave-children wore no clothing at all. Most masters gave each adult bondswoman one gown and provided one shirt and a pair of pants for each adult male slave, but we know of a Virginia slaveholder and a Texas slaveholder who did not give their bondsmen trousers. Louisa Everett's recall was that a shirt was all that the male slaves on the McClain plantation wore.[21] The Texas ex-slave Ben Simpson went naked. He said, "We never had any clothes."[22] Generally, slaves went barefoot in the summer months.[23] According to ex-slave James L. Smith's account, in the winter the typical slaveholder would give his slaves an overcoat or round jacket, a pair of coarse brogan shoes once a year, and a wool hat once every two or three years.[24]

The slave family worked together to provide more clothing for its members. The fugitive slave James W. C. Pennington remembered helping his father to make straw hats and willow baskets, by which means his family purchased more articles of clothing. About these, he stated, "Slaves in the mildest form of the system never get from the master."[25] After bondswomen completed the day's work, they spun, wove, and sewed clothes for their families. An ex-slave from South Carolina, Mary Edwards, said, "We made our own clothes which we done sometimes late in evening."[26] Nancy Boudry recalled as well, "Us had clothes 'cause we spun de thread and weaved 'em."[27]

David Brion Davis observed that slave families "provided a refuge from the dehumanizing effects of being treated as chattel property."[28] They were invaluable to the slave community because they gave their members needed love and compassion. Adult slaves contributed meaningful labor and provided essential material resources such as food and clothing for their children. Serving as family providers allowed the bondsman and the bondswoman to develop identities separate and apart from those assigned to them by their owners, and helped them to gain a sense of personal autonomy and self-worth.

Notes

1. Nathan Irvin Huggins, *Black Odyssey: The Afro-American Ordeal in Slavery* (New York: Pantheon Books, 1977), 165.

2. Thomas H. Jones, *The Experiences of Thomas H. Jones, Who was a Slave for Forty-Three Years* (Boston: Boyin and Chandler, 37 Cornhill, 1862), 5.

3. *Born in Slavery: Slave Narratives from the Federal Writers' Project, 1936-1938,* (Wash., D.C.: Library of Congress, 2001), Indiana Narratives, vol. 5, 29. <memory.loc.gov/ammem/snhtml/snhome> (15 April 2006).

4. David Brion Davis, *Inhuman Bondage: The Rise and Fall of Slavery in the New World* (New York: Oxford University Press, 2006), 201.

5. Deborah Gray White, *Ar'n't I a Woman?: Female Slaves in the Plantation South* (New York: W. W. Norton & Co., 1985), 156.

6. Charles Ball, *Slavery in the United States: A Narrative of the Life and Adventures of Charles Ball* (Lewistown, Pennsylvania, 1836), 79; Solomon Northup, *Twelve Years a Slave: Narrative of Solomon Northup* (Auburn: Derby & Miller, 1853), 169; James L. Smith, *Autobiography of James L. Smith* (Norwich, Conn.: Press of the Bulletin Company, 1881), 8.

7. Frederick Douglass, *Frederick Douglass: The Narrative and Selected Writings.* ed. Michael Meyer (New York: McGraw Hill, 1984), 63.

8. Louis Hughes, *Thirty Years a Slave* (Milwaukee, 1897), 20.

9. Charles Ball, *Slavery in the United States: A Narrative of the Life and Adventures of Charles Ball, a Black Man, Who Lived Forty Years in Maryland, South Carolina and Georgia, as a Slave* (Lewistown, Pa.: J. W. Shugert, 1836), 128.

10. *Born in Slavery: Slave Narratives from the Federal Writers' Project,* Maryland Narratives, vol. 8, 7; *Born in Slavery: Slave Narratives from the Federal Writers' Project,* Ohio Narratives, vol. 12, 22; *Born in Slavery: Slave Narratives from the Federal Writers' Project,* South Carolina Narratives, vol. 14, part 1, 191.

11. *Born in Slavery: Slave Narratives from the Federal Writers' Project,* Georgia Narratives, vol. 4, part 2, 106.

12. *Born in Slavery: Slave Narratives from the Federal Writers' Project,* Georgia Narratives, vol. 4, part 1, 22-23.

13. *Born in Slavery: Slave Narratives from the Federal Writers' Project,* Georgia Narratives, vol. 4, part 1, 302.

14. *Born in Slavery: Slave Narratives from the Federal Writers' Project,* Alabama Narratives, vol. 1, 201.

15. *Born in Slavery: Slave Narratives from the Federal Writers' Project,* Georgia Narratives, vol. 4, part 4, 76; Georgia Narratives, vol. 4, part 1, 41.

16. *Born in Slavery: Slave Narratives from the Federal Writers' Project,* Georgia Narratives, vol. 4, part 1, 308.

17. *Born in Slavery: Slave Narratives from the Federal Writers' Project*, Missouri Narratives, vol. 10, 53.

18. *Born in Slavery: Slave Narratives from the Federal Writers' Project*, South Carolina Narratives, vol. 14, part 1, 191.

19. *Born in Slavery: Slave Narratives from the Federal Writers' Project*, Texas Narratives, vol. 16, part 3, 30.

20. *Born in Slavery: Slave Narratives from the Federal Writers' Project*, Missouri Narratives, vol. 10, 207.

21. *Born in Slavery: Slave Narratives from the Federal Writers' Project*, Florida Narratives, vol. 3, 128.

22. *Born in Slavery: Slave Narratives from the Federal Writers' Project*, Texas Narratives, vol. 16, part 4, 28.

23. *Born in Slavery: Slave Narratives from the Federal Writers' Project*, Georgia Narratives, vol. 4, part 2, 174; *Born in Slavery: Slave Narratives from the Federal Writers' Project*, Ohio Narratives, vol. 12, 51.

24. Smith, *Autobiography of James L. Smith*, 7.

25. James W. C. Pennington, *The Fugitive Blacksmith* (London, 1849), 8-9.

26. *Born in Slavery: Slave Narratives from the Federal Writers' Project*, South Carolina Narratives, vol. 14, part 2, 2.

27. *Born in Slavery: Slave Narratives from the Federal Writers' Project*, Georgia Narratives, vol. 4, part 1, 115.

28. Davis, *Inhuman Bondage*, 201.

CHAPTER SIXTEEN

The Break-Up of Marital Unions through Slave Sales

Historians do not agree on whether or not the slaveholder's practice of breaking up slave marital unions through slave sales was widespread. Fogel and Engerman maintained that about 84% of the slaves engaged in the westward trek migrated with their owners.[1] They argued that "the interregional slave trade resulted in the destruction of some slave marriages," but "[d]ata contained in sales records in New Orleans . . . sharply contradict the popular view that the destruction of slave marriages was at least a frequent consequence of the slave trade." Drawing upon records covering thousands of transactions during the years from 1804 to 1862, they found that more than 84% of all sales of slaves who were fourteen years of age or older involved unmarried individuals. Of those married individuals sold, they noted that 6% were sold with their spouses, and probably at least a quarter of the remainder were widowed or voluntarily separated. Fogel and Engerman concluded that "13%, or less, of interregional sales resulted in the destruction of slave marriages. And since sales were only 16% of the total interregional movement, it is probable that only about 2% of the marriages of slaves involved in westward trek were destroyed by the process of migration."[2] If we relied on their records, we might reasonably deduce that slaveholders and traders were concerned about the stability of slave marriages.

Herbert Gutman, however, challenged Fogel and Engerman's interpretation of the New Orleans data. He maintained that the scant information contained in the records kept of slave transfers in interregional markets such as New Orleans did not show the effect of sales on either slave families or slave marriages.[3] Gutman determined that the records were incomplete because the slave sale invoices indicated no more than a slave's age and sex. He pointed out the pitfalls of using that evidence as clues to the slave family structure.[4]

Even if the data had identified married slaves as well, it probably still would have been an inaccurate measure of dissolved slave unions because it would not have taken into account unmarried slaves who had lived together as life-long companions.

A focus on slaves "married" in the conventional sense is pointless in any debate over whether or not the dissolution of ante-bellum-era slave unions was a frequent consequence of the slave trade. Held as property, the slaves had no legal capacity to assent to any contract—including a contract of matrimony. "Legal marriages," the historian Charles H. Nichols wrote, "would have been an offense to the owner's . . . licentious appetite."[5] Sarah Ross, a former slave from Mississippi, told us that enslaved black men and women in the ante-bellum South did not marry; they cohabited "in many cases against their will . . . as man and wife."[6] The Georgia ex-slave Elsie Moreland recalled that her sister and a male companion "just lived together, 'cause that's the way they done in them days."[7] A slave may have referred to his union as a marriage, but it is more accurately called a contubernium—a permitted co-habitation of slaves to which no legal rights were attached.

That many of the slaves who were recorded in sale invoices in markets such as New Orleans were not listed as married reveals nothing about whether or not they were bonded in monogamous unions when slave traders sold them. If asked whether or not they were married, some slaves probably would have responded in the negative. For example, when an interviewer asked Georgia Baker whether she was married or not, she replied, "Lawdy Miss! I ain't never been married, but I did live wid Major Baker eighteen years and us had five chillun."[8] No doubt separation from a companion would have been as traumatic for an unmarried bondswoman like Georgia Baker as for one whose sale invoice had indicated that she was married.

Studies have been conducted on the effect of slave sales on the slave family and, more specifically, slave marriages. In response to Fogel and Engerman's contention that only 13% or fewer of interregional sales resulted in the destruction of slave marriages, Herbert Gutman produced statistics of his own that showed a higher percentage of dissolved slave marriages. Using marriage registration books kept by the Union Army clergy in Davis Bend, Natchez, and Vicksburg, Mississippi and recorded in 1864-65, Gutman estimated that 17% of the recorded marriages were broken up by slaveowners and traders. He found that an even higher percentage of black slaves twenty years and older (nearly one in six registrants) had been separated from a companion by force and nearly one in four men and one in five women aged thirty or older had suffered such a separation. Forcible separations were significant among younger slaves as well. Gutman estimated that one in ten men and women born between the years 1835 and 1845 had experienced forcible separation by the year 1864. From his sources, he found that percentages were high enough to conclude that even in the pre-Civil War decade, "the peculiar institution retained the grimmest quality; the break-up of marriages and the damage these inflicted on the husbands and wives . . . ."[9]

Other historians claim that slave traders destroyed an even higher percentage of slave marriages through slave sales. John Blassingame used a different source of information which, in his opinion, was the best objective evidence available and found slave sales responsible for forcibly dissolving 32.4% of black unions. [10] Peter Kolchin estimated that slave sales broke up one in every three slave marriages as well. [11] All of these studies, considered together, suggest that the slaveowner and trader's practice of breaking up slave marriages was widespread. During the ante-bellum period, probably between 25% and 33% of all slave unions were forcibly dissolved by slave sales.

In their narratives, former slaves tell us that slave-trading severed countless marital bonds. The Georgia ex-slave Amanda McDaniel recalled that her mother, Matilda Hale, was snatched from her first husband, sold to a slave trader in Virginia, and eventually sold along with her two youngest children to a Georgia slaveholder. [12] Sojourner Truth was married to a former slave named Thomas who had twice married previously. She noted that one of his wives, if not both, had been separated from him and sold far away. Truth added, "And it was more than probable that he was not only allowed but encouraged to take another at each successive sale. . . . Such is the custom among slaveholders at the present day." [13] The former slave Samuel Ringgold Ward was mindful that "marriage must succumb to slavery; slavery must reign supreme over every right and institution, however venerable or sacred." [14]

In all the slaveholding states except Louisiana, [15] no restriction of any kind prevented the violent separation of husbands from wives or parents from children. [16] On February 7, 1839, in a speech before the United States Senate, Senator Henry Clay in fact said, "The moment that the incontestable fact is admitted, that the slaves are property, the law of movable property irresistibly attaches itself to them, and secures the right of carrying them from one State to another." [17]

Southern white planters saw owning slaves as a convenient way to move wealth from state-to-state. [18] Slaveholders and traders separated slave-spouses from one another; but more often, they separated slave-fathers from their children. [19] The slave-husband and father's removal from a state and his separation from his loved ones, for him, produced emotionally and psychologically devastating consequences. Charles Ball never forgot the emotional trauma and depression he suffered when his master sold him from his wife and children. In the following passage, he laments the loss of his family:

> This man came up to me and, seizing me by the collar, shook me violently, saying I was his property, and must go with him to Georgia. At the sound of these words, the thoughts of my wife and children rushed across my mind. . . . I saw and knew my case was hopeless, and that resistance was in vain . . . . I asked if I could not be allowed to see my wife and children, or if this could not be permitted, if they might not leave them to come see me; but I was told that I would be able to get another wife in Georgia. . . . I became very wary of life and bitterly execrated the day I was born. . . . I longed to die. . . . If I could have got a rope I should have hanged myself at Lancaster. [20]

More concerned with their economic well-being, many slaveholders were not interested in promoting stable relationships in the slave quarters. The South placed laws on the books, elevating slaveholder property interests over slave marital interests. As the Southerner R. Q. Mallard wrote, "In too many instances the marriage relation was broken up, not often voluntarily."[21] Slaveholders severed slave marital bonds in the interest of profit.

The Master's Rationale for Encouraging Stable Slave Unions

When masters did promote stable slave marital arrangements, they did not do so out of any moral concern. Generally, slaveholders encouraged slaves to pair off in order to create more slave labor, maintain discipline and social control, and discourage runaways. As Angela Davis forcefully insists, bonds they "allowed to thrive were, for the most part, external fabrications serving the designs of an avaricious, profit-seeking slaveholder."[22]

Many slaveholders who encouraged slaves to marry did so because they knew that pairing slaves would have insured a steady supply of new slaves. In 1832, Thomas R. Dew explained that the slaveholder's chief rationale for wanting his slaves to marry was to increase his slave holdings. He observed that the ban on the Atlantic Slave Trade furnished "every inducement to the master to attend to his Negroes and encourage marriage, and to cause the greatest possible number to be raised, and thus it affords a powerful stimulus to the spring of black population . . . ."[23] In 1853, Reverend William Goodell noted as well that the masters in the ante-bellum South licensed their bondswomen to be "breeders," not wives.[24] Thus, as Henry H. Butler told us, the most important factor in securing a slaveholder's consent to a slave marriage would have been that slaveowner's desire to rear slaves with perfect physiques.[25] Indeed, we may gather that if a physically robust bondsman were to have requested permission from a slaveholder to marry one of his slavewoman, eager to own more healthy slave-children, that master probably would have granted it without delay.[26]

The ex-slave Andrew Jackson recalled that his master told him "to 'get married' according to slavery, or in other words, to enrich his plantation by a family of young slaves." Jackson's sole option was to be sold to a slave trader who was making up a slave gang for a market further south.[27] Henry Bibb intimated that his wife's owner gave him permission to marry on the condition that he father slave-children. He wrote,

> Malinda's master was very much in favor of the match, but entirely upon selfish principles. When I went to ask his permission to marry Malinda, his answer was in the affirmative but with one condition, which I consider too vulgar to be written in this book.[28]

John Blassingame, among others, found that other slaveholders avoided dissolving slave marital unions to maintain discipline.[29] When it came to the purchase of slaves, the exceptional more humane masters—perhaps reluctant to bullwhip their disobedient slaves—were aware of the potential discipline problem the involuntarily dissolution of a slave marriage might cause. Concerned that a slave named Dick was likely to be troublesome without his family, the slaveholder James Mercer purchased the slave's wife and children.[30] Masters realized that slaves who were emotionally tied to companions were less likely to run away as well.

Notes

1. Robert W. Fogel and Stanley L. Engerman, *Time on the Cross* (Boston: Little, Brown & Co., 1974), 48.

2. Fogel and Engerman, *Time on the Cross*, 49.

3. Herbert G. Gutman, *The Black Family in Slavery and Freedom 1750-1925* (New York: Vintage Books, 1977), 145.

4. Herbert G. Gutman, *Slavery and the Numbers Game* (Chicago: University of Illinois Press, 1975), 142-57. Similarly, Paul A. David *et al.* are credited for exposing Fogel and Engerman's tactics of distortion and selective inattention. Paul A. David, *et al., Reckoning With Slavery: Critical Essays in the Quantitative History of the American Negro* (New York: Oxford University Press, 1976).

5. Charles H. Nichols, *Many Thousand Gone: The Ex-Slaves' Account of Their Bondage and Freedom* (Leiden, Netherlands: E. J. Brill, 1963), 36.

6. *Born in Slavery: Slave Narratives from the Federal Writers' Project, 1936-1938,* (Wash., D.C.: Library of Congress, 2001), Florida Narratives, vol. 3, 168. <memory.loc.gov/ammem/snhtml/snhome> (15 April 2006).

7. Andrew Waters, ed., *On Jordan's Stormy Banks* (Winston-Salem, N.C.: John F. Blair, Publisher 2000), 136.

8. George P. Rawick, ed., *The American Slave: A Composite Autobiography*, 41 vols. (Westport, Conn.: Greenwood Publishing Co., 1972), Georgia, part 1, 50.

9. Gutman, *Black Family in Slavery and Freedom*, 146.

10. Blassingame wrote,

> The best objective evidence available concerning the separation of mates by planters appears in the marriage certificates of former slaves reserved by the Union Army and the Freedmen's Bureau in Tennessee (Dyer, Gibson, Wilson and Shelby counties), Louisiana (Concordia Parish), and Mississippi (Adams County) from 1864-66 . . . . Marriage certificates contain revealing data on 2,888 slave unions in three states; 1,225 in Mississippi, 1,123 in Tennessee, and 540 in Louisiana. The callous attitudes frequently held by planters toward slave unions are revealed clearly in the statistics: 937 or 32.4% of the unions were dissolved by masters. The overwhelming majority of the couples were separated before they reached their sixth anniversary.

John W. Blassingame, *The Slave Community* (New York: Oxford University Press, 1972), 175-77.

11. Peter Kolchin, *American Slavery 1619-1877* (New York: Hill and Wang, 1993), 125-26.

12. *Born in Slavery: Slave Narratives from the Federal Writers' Project*, Georgia Narratives, vol. 4, part 3, 71-75.

13. Sojourner Truth, *Narrative of Sojourner Truth* (New York: Arno Press, 1968), 36.

14. Samuel Ringgold Ward, *Autobiography of a Fugitive Negro: His Anti-Slavery Labours in the United States, Canada & England* (1855; reprinted New York: Arno Press and the New York Times, 1968), 16.

15. Two reasons are apparent. First, slaves in other states were chattel—an article of movable personal property; in Louisiana, slaves were held as real estate and were therefore immovable. Second, a Louisiana law enacted in 1806 prohibited the public sale of disabled slaves (either because of age or other reasons) from their children and prohibited the sale of a child under the age of ten separately from his mother. William Goodell, *The American Slave Code in Theory and Practice: Its Distinctive Features Shown by Its Statutes, Judicial Decisions, and Illustrative Facts* (New York: American and Foreign Anti-Slavery Society, 1853) part 1, ch. 2, 46-47; Thomas D. Morris, *Southern Slavery and the Law: 1619 – 1860* (Chapel Hill: University of North Carolina Press, 1996), 77.

16. Frederic Bancroft, *Slave Trading in the Old South* (Baltimore, Md.: J. H. Furst Company, 1931; reprinted, New York: Fredrick Unger Publishing Company, 1959), 199.

17. Goodell, *The American Slave Code*, part 1, ch. 2, 48.

18. Nathan Irvin Huggins, *Black Odyssey: The Afro-American Ordeal in Slavery* (New York: Pantheon Books, 1977), 115.

19. Deborah Gray White, *Ar'n't I a Woman?: Female Slaves in the Plantation South* (New York: W. W. Norton & Co., 1985), 145.

20. Charles Ball, *Slavery in the United States: A Narrative of the Life and Adventures of Charles Ball* (Lewistown, Pa.: J. W. Shugert, 1836), 29-35.

21. R.Q. Mallard, D. D., *Plantation Life before Emancipation* (Richmond, Va.: Whittet and Shepperson, 1892), 48.

22. Angela Davis, "Reflections on the Black Woman's Role in the Community of Slaves," *Black Scholar* 3 (Dec. 1971): 4.

23. *The Pro-Slavery Argument as Maintained by the Most Distinguished Writers of the Southern States* (Charleston: Walker, Richards and Company, 1852), 473.

24. Goodell, *The American Slave Code*, part 1, ch. 7, 106.

25. *Born in Slavery: Slave Narratives from the Federal Writers' Project*, Texas Narratives, vol. 16, 180.

26. *Born in Slavery: Slave Narratives from the Federal Writers' Project*, Texas Narratives, vol. 16, part 2, 57.

27. Andrew Jackson, *Narrative and Writings of Andrew Jackson* (Syracuse, N.Y., 1827), 8.

28. Henry Bibb, *Narrative of the Life and Adventures of Henry Bibb, an American Slave* (New York, 1849), 79.

29. Blassingame, *The Slave Community*, 173.

30. Gerald W. Mullin, *Flight and Rebellion* (New York: Oxford University Press, 1972), 27.

CHAPTER SEVENTEEN

The Promiscuous Bondswoman: Myth or Reality?

During the ante-bellum period, was the promiscuous bondswoman a myth or a reality? Was the enslaved black woman actually indiscriminate in her choice of bed partners and guilty of taking on multiple ones, or was that merely an image created by circumstances having nothing to do with her voluntary sexual activity? Much has been written about the so-called sexual promiscuity of black bondswomen.[1] Fogel and Engerman, for example, say that the presence of large numbers of "tawny, golden, and white or nearly white" slaves was "proof beyond denial of either the ubiquity of the exploitation of black women by white men, or of the promiscuity of black women, or of both."[2]

While it is true that slaveholders encouraged and—in many instances as we have seen—compelled Africans in the ante-bellum South to increase their slave labor supply by having children, and also true that slaves were not allowed to make legal marriage contracts, it appears equally true from the testimony of former slaves that most enslaved blacks did not voluntarily breed promiscuously. If the promiscuous bondswoman was just an image, was that image the white Southerner's misconception or his invention, or a combination of the two?

At this point, we should defer to the sharp insight of Deborah Gray White. She attributed what she called "one of the most prevalent images of black women in ante-bellum America"—the "Jezebel character," a woman "governed almost entirely by her libido"—to the fact that bondswomen were often semi-clad. White argued that many ante-bellum white Southerners were influenced by the mid-nineteenth-century ideal of the Victorian lady, a respectable white woman covered by layers of clothing and never exposing "even her legs and arms to public view without arousing the ire of her husband and the contempt of her community." Based on this ideal they determined that the bondswoman's semi-nudity was conclusive evidence of her promiscuity.[3] Thus, the characterization of the bondswoman as promiscuous was a dubious inference at best.

White found that some bondswomen wore tattered clothes, rendering them almost naked, and others were exposed because of the type of work they performed—particularly those slave-women on rice plantations who "worked in water with their dresses 'reefed up' around their hips, exposing their legs and thighs."[4] Slave buyers exposed other bondwomen's bodies when they examined them on the auction block. An ex-slave from Arkansas, Julia Grace, recalled that when slave traders put her mother and other slave-women on the auction block, they would weigh them, strip them naked to see if there was anything wrong with them and how they were built, and then bid them off.[5] Having seen many slaves sold on the auction block, Andrew Boone also told us, "Dey would strip 'em stark naked."[6]

Slaveholders stripped bondswomen to the waist when they whipped them as well.[7] Susan Hamilton's recall was that the slaveholder whipped the slave-woman "with only sumpin' tied 'round her lower parts of de body."[8] Amanda Ross, a former slave from Arkansas, similarly stated that she saw "'em tie the women up, strip 'em naked to their waist and whip 'em till the blood run down their backs."[9] Simply stated, the typical bondswoman was not willingly indiscriminate in her choice of bed partners; the revealing clothing that she wore may have helped to foster the false, unflattering image of what White called "a woman obsessed with matters of the flesh."[10]

White maintained that some ante-bellum white Southerners regarded the high birth rates among bondswomen as evidence of their promiscuity.[11] As previously pointed out, however, many engaged in sexual intercourse against their will. Even the son of a Virginia slaveholder, Moncure D. Conway, was constrained by conscience to write, "I grieve to say that there is too much ground for the charges that general licentiousness among the slaves, for the purpose of a large increase, is compelled by some masters."[12] If slaveholders forced bondswomen to procreate under the threat of death, injury, or sale, surely those who labeled them sexually promiscuous for bearing many children unfairly mischaracterized them; their owners controlled their reproductive schedules.

Angela Davis holds a different view on the origin of the image of the promiscuous bondswoman. She insists that the image—like its twin image, the black rapist—was a white Southerner's invention. In her opinion, Southern whites created the promiscuous bondswoman to apologize for and facilitate their continued sexual exploitation of black women.[13] Unfortunately, even relatively enlightened observers during the ante-bellum period misunderstood the sexual attitudes of enslaved blacks. Current social scientists have misconceptions as well.

Since the vast majority of slaves who were brought to America came from West Africa, what, if any, impact did traditional West African culture have on the slave in shaping his attitude toward sex?[14] The scholar Jacques Maquet noted, "African sexuality both in and out of marriage shows moderation and control."[15] He added, "The African idea of sexuality avoids dramatizing and personalizing this activity as we have been taught to do so by romantic tradition."[16] Determined largely by extended kinship networks and religious obligations, the African's attitude toward sex differed greatly from those current at the time in Europe. Traditional West African societies viewed sex as natural, as something fundamental to procreation and a religious duty to insure continuation of the family lineage established by their ancestors. Furthermore, since barrenness was a calamity in Africa, great value was placed on fertility and procreation.

Excepting the Hausa and the Nupe of Nigeria, most African societies considered pre-marital chastity of no importance because they did not regard pre-marital sex as something dirty or sinful, or as an impulse to be suppressed. They accepted it as a normal part of the courtship process. Polygamy was a cultural tradition, but extramarital sex was not tolerated and—unlike the Southern slaveholding class—traditional West African societies generally forbade incest. But many mid-nineteenth-century observers, influenced by Victorian mores, believed pre-marital sex to be evidence of the absence of sexual standards and of savage behavior. They found sexual morality synonymous with sexual restraint and considered sex appropriate only after marriage. These views probably helped to create misconceptions regarding the sexual attitudes of Africans in America as well.

For the slaves, voluntary sexual relations were almost always followed by permanent bonds and were hardly evidence of indiscriminate mating. Asked what proportion of slave-women voluntarily had sexual intercourse before marriage, the ex-slave Robert Smalls replied, "The majority do but they do not consider this intercourse an evil thing."[17] Generally speaking, it was a prelude to a permanent bond, whether or not we choose to call the union a marriage. If the bondswoman's new lover did not accept her as a wife, another man would have accepted her even if she had "outside" children, and the slave community would not have stigmatized those children because of the pre-marital sexual activity of their parents.

Thomas H. Jones, a former slave, understood the value of monogamous arrangements. He wanted a companion whom he "could love with all his warm affections and who would love [him] in return." He desired a partner of whom he "might think when toiling for a selfish unfeeling master," who would "dwell fondly on [his] memory when [they] were separated during the severe labors of the day," and with whom he "might enjoy the blessed happiness of social endearments after the work of each day was over."[18] Lewis Clarke, a fugitive slave from Kentucky, saw many bondswomen sobbing and crying for their mates sold to slaveholders in the Deep South.[19] Married or unmarried, slaves developed strong emotional ties to their partners and consequently lamented the loss of their beloved companions.

Driven purely by materialism and blind to the misery consequent upon the arbitrary destruction of such unions, many masters simply compelled the unfortunate spouses to take other partners or suffer the consequences of torture or sale. William Wells Brown wrote about slaveholders who sold slave-husbands from their wives and compelled the wives to take other husbands. When he asked a slave-woman named Sally why she married a slave named Peter so soon after they sold her first husband, she replied, "Because master made me do it."[20]

Generally, if a slave lost a spouse, he would have mourned for that companion and would not have married soon after unless driven by want. Eventually, the slave might have found a new partner. The South Carolina ex-slave Sylvia Durant recalled that a slaveholder sold her uncle's wife and a speculator carried her mother's first husband off, but both her uncle and her mother eventually re-married.[21] Thomas H. Jones undoubtedly experienced bitterness and agony when a slaveholder separated him from his first wife and children, but out of a yearning for affection he took another wife. He wrote,

> The memory . . . will find a fresh impression on my heart while that heart shall beat. . . . I passed four years, and I began to feel that I could not live in utter loneliness any longer. My heart was still and always yearning for affection . . . and loving communion . . . . I asked Mary R. Moore to come and cheer me in my desolate home . . . . She is now my wife and she is with me today and till death part us.[22]

Having lost a long-time companion through sale, even the most committed of slaves understood the value of monogamous unions as important survival mechanisms. Many slaves were driven by want to find new partners; however, they could not rest assured that those unions would never be severed as a result of the sale of their new mates. Interviewed in the 1850s about his separation from his wives, a slave from Weldon, North Carolina stated, "I had twelve [children] by my firs' wife. I got her when I was sixteen, and lived wid her for twenty-four years. Den da sold her and all de chil'ren." Five years later, he and another woman jumped over the broom, but he lived with that wife a little more than three years when his master sold her away.[23] The slaves' personal accounts are a testament to the importance to them of such monogamous unions and to the emotional damage inflicted on slave-partners who were separated from each other through sale.

Notes

1. E. Franklin Frazier, *Negro Family in the United States* (Chicago: University of Chicago Press, 1939), 19-21, 78.

2. Robert W. Fogel and Stanley L. Engerman, *Time on the Cross* (Boston: Little, Brown & Co., 1974), 131-32.

3. Deborah Gray White, *Ar'n't I a Woman?: Female Slaves in the Plantation* (New York: W. W. Norton & Co., 1985), 29-33.

4. White, *Ar'n't I a Woman?* 29-33.

5. *Born in Slavery: Slave Narratives from the Federal Writers' Project, 1936-1938* (Wash., D.C.: Library of Congress, 2001), Arkansas Narratives, vol. 2, part 3, 65. <memory.loc.gov/ammem/snhtml/snhome> (15 April 2006).

6. *Born in Slavery: Slave Narratives from the Federal Writers' Project*, North Carolina Narratives, vol. 11, part 1, 133.

7. White, *Ar'n't I a Woman?* 29-33.

8. George P. Rawick, ed., *The American Slave: A Composite Autobiography*, 41 vols. (Westport, Conn.: Greenwood Publishing Co., 1972), South Carolina, part 2, 27.

9. *Born in Slavery: Slave Narratives from the Federal Writers' Project*, Arkansas Narratives, vol. 2, part 6, 80.

10. White, *Ar'n't I a Woman?* 46.

11. White, *Ar'n't I a Woman?* 31.

12. Frederic Bancroft, *Slave Trading in the Old South* (Baltimore, Md.: J. H. Furst Company, 1931; reprinted, New York: Fredrick Unger Publishing Company, 1959), 76; Bancroft obtained the quote from *Testimonies Concerning Slavery* (2d ed., London, 1865), 20.

13. Angela Y. Davis, *Women, Race & Class* (New York: Vintage Books, 1983), 174.

14. John Hope Franklin and Alfred A. Moss, Jr., *From Slavery to Freedom*, 6th Ed. (New York: Alfred A. Knopf, Inc., 1988), 39.

15. Jacques Maquet, *Africanity: The Cultural Unity of Black Africa* (New York: Oxford University Press, 1972), 75.

16. Maquet, *Africanity*, 75.

17. Herbert G. Gutman, *The Black Family in Slavery and Freedom* (New York: Vintage Books, 1977), 63.

18. Thomas H. Jones, *The Experiences of Thomas H. Jones, Who was a Slave for Forty-Three Years* (Boston: Boyin and Chandler, 37 Cornhill, 1862), 30.

19. John W. Blassingame, *Slave Testimony* (Baton Rouge: Louisiana State University Press, 1977), 160.

20. William Wells Brown, *Narrative of William Wells Brown, a Fugitive Slave, Now in England,* (Boston, 1847), 89.

21. *Born in Slavery: Slave Narratives from the Federal Writers' Project*, South Carolina Narratives, vol. 14, part 1, 342.

22. Jones, *The Experiences of Thomas H. Jones*, 30.

23. James Redpath, *The Roving Editor: Or Talks with Slaves in the Southern States,* (New York: A. B. Burdick Publisher, 1859), 117.

CHAPTER EIGHTEEN

The Break-Up of Slave Families

"The Slave Mother"

She is a mother, pale with fear,
Her boy clings to her side,
And in her kirtle vainly tries
His trembling form to hide.
He is not hers, although she bore
For him a mother's pain;
He is not hers, although her blood
Is coursing through his veins!

—FRANCES E. W. HARPER,
Poems on Miscellaneous Subjects, 1854

Undoubtedly, the domestic slave trade destroyed innumerable slave families. Slaveholders created an intricate system of domestic slave-trading before the demise of the Atlantic Slave Trade. In the last half of the eighteenth century, it was well-developed—particularly in the Atlantic seaboard states of the Carolinas, Maryland, and Virginia. The historian Frederic Bancroft cited advertisements in daily newspapers as evidence of that development. A February 25, 1796 Charleston, South Carolina newspaper, for example, contained fourteen slave sale ads about the public or private sale, hiring, or purchase of 288 slaves, and not one of those slaves came directly either from Africa or another state.[1] In his study of Maryland slaves, Allan Kulikoff found that even on large plantations social life was insecure and slaves were sold away from their loved ones. He estimated that about 20% of all slaves in southern Maryland left the region between the years 1755 and 1782.[2]

The greatest demand for slaves came from Louisiana, Mississippi, Alabama, and Texas, as well as Georgia, Tennessee, and Missouri. In Virginia, Maryland, and Kentucky, where slaveholders found slave labor less remunerative, they deemed the rearing of slaves for sale most important. As Frederic Bancroft pointed out,

> [After 1820,] the decline in the value of land and crops, except for the best tobacco, was so great in Virginia that only the demand for "Virginia leaf" and the sale of surplus negroes [rapidly increasing in price] to the Southern cotton-planters enabled the inhabitants to keep the wolf from the door and to maintain a semblance of their former hospitality.[3]

After the end of the Atlantic Slave Trade in 1808, in the District of Columbia the increase in slave prices gave more economic incentive to shrewd calculating slaveholders, and they increasingly sold from their slave families the members reared among them. In the South, the period from the 1820s forward was conducive to selling slaves. If the slaveholders overlooked that fact, the slave traders constantly reminded them of it. The historian Frederic Bancroft wrote,

> When the slave owners did not seek out traders and request that "high price in cash," the impatient traders went to the markets to look for masters that might be tempted. A Southwestern trader would give much more cash for a prime field hand or a young women with one or two children than the average Maryland or Virginia farmer could save from years of agriculture labor. And selling at such a time enabled the vendor to explain matters at home to suit himself.[4]

Domestic slave-trading actually reached its peak in the 1830s.[5] During that period, the slave population in Maryland decreased by about 13%.[6] If we look at the census figures for that state for the period from 1830 to 1840, we can see the effect slave-trading had on that population. Eighteen of the nineteen Maryland counties for which we have data experienced decreases in the slave population; the total decrease was over 14,000 slaves. The following are the census figures[7] for those counties:

TABLE 18.1: MARYLAND'S SLAVE POPULATION

Maryland Counties	*Slave Populations*	
	1830	1840
Allegany	818	812
Anne Arundel	10,347	9,819
Baltimore	10,653	7,595
Calvert	3,899	4,170

Caroline	1,177	752
Cecil	1,705	1,352
Charles	10,129	9,182
Dorchester	5,001	4,227
Frederick	6,370	4,445
Harford	2,947	2,643
Kent	3,191	2,735
Montgomery	6,447	5,377
Prince George's	11,585	10,636
Queen Anne	4,872	3,960
Saint Mary's	6,183	5,761
Somerset	6,556	5,377
Talbot	4,173	3,687
Washington	2,909	2,546
Worchester	<u>2,546</u>	<u>3,539</u>
TOTAL	102,994	88,615

William Calderhead conducted a study of slave sales for the years from 1830 to 1840 in eight Maryland counties.[8] The slave population of those counties in the year 1830 totaled 46,840. He found that during that ten-year period 1,991 slave sales involving the sale of 5,073 slaves occurred.[9] Having interpreted Calderhead's study, Herbert Gutman concluded that the volume of sales had an effect on the slave family, but that the exact effect could not be known. "If the average slave family in 1830 had four members," wrote Gutman, "then there were 17 sales per 100 families and 43 slaves sold per 100 families."[10]

The Commonwealth of Virginia led all Atlantic seaboard states in the number of slaves traded. Although the Virginia slave population decreased by only about 4% during that same ten-year period, the total decrease was more than 20,000 slaves.[11] In fact, Kenneth Stampp estimated that in the last three decades of the ante-bellum era nearly 300,000 Virginia slaves were transported to the Deep South.[12]

During the Virginia legislative debates of 1832 concerning the abolition of slavery, both slavery proponents and abolitionists agreed that slave-rearing was a common means of profit and slave traders took thousands of Virginia slaves to the Southwest. Addressing the legislature, Thomas R. Dew stated, "From all the information we can obtain, we have no hesitation in saying that upwards of 6,000 are yearly exported to other states." He added, "Virginia is, in fact, a Negro raising state for other states; she produces enough for her own supply, and 6,000 for sale."[13] Frederic Bancroft estimated that between the years 1830 and 1840, Virginia's yearly export of slaves was almost twice that; he found that the Commonwealth annually exported approximately 11,800 slaves.[14]

Although much of the growth of the slave population during that ten-year period was natural and in large part the result of the slaveholder's practice of slave breeding, while the Maryland and Virginia slave populations decreased, the slave population further south increased. The Georgia and Tennessee slave populations grew by about 30% and Louisiana's grew more than 50%. The slave populations in Alabama and Missouri more than doubled, the slave population in Mississippi increased almost threefold, and the one in Arkansas grew more than fourfold.[15] We know that slaves imported from Maryland and Virginia constituted much of the increase in those populations.

That the states of Maryland and Virginia annually exported thousands of slaves suggests that slaveholders were not averse to breaking up slave families for profit, and that the number of families destroyed by sales was sufficiently high to inflict emotional trauma on thousands of slave family members. Indeed, Charles H. Nichols correctly observed that "perhaps the most inhuman phase of the slave trade" was the unavoidable separation of slave families.[16]

Although slaveholders, other defenders of the American slavery regime, and even some social scientists denied its widespread occurrence, the selling of slave-children from their families was a disturbing fact of slave life.[17] Since most slaveholders viewed the birth of a slave-child as an economic event, the time at which they sold slave-children from their families depended not on the children's psychological or emotional preparedness for separation, but on their salability, the economic needs of the slaveholder, and the degree of market pressure.[18]

Peter Kolchin estimated that almost half of all slave-children were separated from at least one parent.[19] The practice of separating them from their families was most frequent following the death of a slaveholder and during periods of financial stress. The parents could do nothing to prevent it. In fact, the South Carolinian observer Angelina Grimke Weld noted that they had as little control over the sale of their children "as have domestic animals over the disposal of their young."[20] Charles Ball's mother and several of her children were sold to separate purchasers upon his master's death.[21] The former slave Lunsford Lane recalled that his mistress sold a number of her slaves from their families and friends and sold several children from their parents after his master died.[22]

Another time at which slaveholders separated slave-children from their families was when they gave them away as bridal gifts to their children. Dr. George Washington Buckner's sister was given away as a bridal gift to his master's daughter. Asked how he felt about it, Dr. Buckner replied, "It always filled us with sorrow when we were separated either by circumstance of marriage or death."[23]

Other slaveholders threatened to sell slave-children from their parents to maintain discipline and control. A former slave from North Carolina, Clara Jones, told us that right after she bore her fifth child, she fell out in the field—apparently from exhaustion. She said that her master "ain't had but about fifty slaves but he makes dem do de work of a hundred an' fifty." Her owner went out to the field, kicked her, and warned her that if she did not get up and work he was going to sell her ten-month-old baby.[24]

How did the slave community deal with the parentless slave-child? Similarities can be seen in the adaptive mechanisms traditional West African societies made use of during the absence of a child's parents. In traditional West African societies, the concept "orphan" generally did not exist. In the event of a parent's death, an African child had only to mingle in his village to see several relatives who would substitute for his mother, father, brothers, and sisters—and they would treat him accordingly.[25] The slave community retained those West African adaptive mechanisms. In the slave quarters, there were many children separated from their parents, siblings, or other relatives. Under those circumstances, familial arrangements in the slave quarters worked against isolation. As a matter of course, unattached children were assimilated into other slave families.

Although acceptance by other families in the slave quarters probably helped the child to adjust, it probably did not mitigate the initial emotional trauma of being separated from parents and other loved ones. Delia Garlic had thirteen siblings but knew only one; her masters separated her from them all and eventually sold her from her mother. She said, "Babies was snatched from deir mother's breast and sold to speculators. Chillens was separated from sisters and brothers and never saw each other again." Asked whether or not the children cried when they were separated, Garlic replied, "'Course dey cry. You think they not cry when dey was sold like cattle? I could tell you about it all day, but even den you couldn't guess de awfulness of it."[26]

Certain slave-children might have been sold only a few miles away, but when slaveholders sold them, their destinations were routinely concealed from their parents. It would have been difficult for their parents to find them, for the names of slaves were commonly changed with every change of their owners. Moses Grandy observed, "Slaves usually bear the name of the master to whom they belong at the time; they have no family name of their own by which they can be traced."[27]

Although ownership of the slave-child belonged to the owner of that child's mother, and though the mother was less likely than the father to be separated from her children, that should not diminish the fact that slaveholders also frequently separated slave-children from their mothers. James L. Smith recalled that the first cruel act of his master was to sell his sister Cella. He noted that his mother "bore this shock in silent but bitter agony."[28] Linda Brent saw a slave-mother lead seven of her children to the auction block. She wrote the following:

She knew that *some* of them would be taken from her; but they took *all*. The children were sold to a slave-trader, and their mother bought by a man in her town. Before night her children were all far away. She begged the trader to tell her where he intended to take them; this he refused to do. How *could* he, when he knew he would sell them one by one, wherever he could command the highest price? I met that mother in the street, and her wild, haggard face lives today in my mind. She wrung her hands in anguish, and exclaimed, "Gone! All gone! Why *don't* God kill me?" I had no words wherewith to comfort her. Instances of this kind are daily, yea, of hourly occurrence.[29]

Since the break-up of the slave family was a function of economics calculated in money and goods, the best plan for effecting good sales was to put up each slave-child separately at auction, sometimes giving a few days notice. Frederic Bancroft found that the "selling singly of young children privately and publicly was frequent and notorious."[30] Moses Grandy, for example, told us that although one of his sisters was sold away from her husband with an infant at her breast, four of her six children were sold away one at a time.[31] William Wells Brown's mother and all her children were sold to different slaveholders in the city of St. Louis.[32]

Frederic Bancroft observed that, excepting slave-mothers and their small children—and often only some of them—it was common for slaveholders and traders to divide slave families.[33] He wrote,

> When it was expected to be markedly advantageous, the everyday practice in selling slaves to pay debts and settle estates was to divide families, often excepting mother and children. The fact that the law did not prohibit such separations, but sanctioned and even compelled them when parties in interest demanded them; that the interstate traders were suspected of intending to divide families when they advertised for them; that all but a small percentage of slaves they had for sale were "single" or young mothers with small children, and that the slaves in the markets, unless in gangs from estates, were almost exclusively of the same kind. . . these and many other facts to be duly noticed, are conclusive evidence that it was common to divide families.[34]

His conclusion finds support in the testimony of former slaves. Sarah Byrd, a Virginia ex-slave, said, "Chile, in them days so many families were broke up and some went one way and der others went t'other way; and you nebber seed them no more. Virginia was a reg'lar slave market."[35] Lewis Clarke was thoroughly convinced that the slaveholders minded "no more selling children away from a slave than they [did] calves from a cow."[36] One slave-mother named Charity worked years to buy her son from his mistress, only to be told by the mistress that she had sold him. She recalled the following:

> I wanted to keep the right side of her, in hopes that she'd let me have my boy. One day she sent me on an errand . . . When I came back mistress was counting a heap of bills in her lap. She was a rich women—she rolled in gold. My little girl stood behind the chair and the mistress counted the money — ten

dollars — twenty dollars — fifty dollars — I see that she kept crying. I thought that maybe the mistress had struck her . . . . I went up to her and whispered, "What's the matter?" She pointed to mistress' lap and said, "Broder's money! Broder's money!" Oh, then I understood it all! I said to mistress McKinley, "Have you sold my boy?" Without looking up from counting her money, she drawled out, "Yes Charity; I got a great price for him!"[37]

Historians of American slavery generally agree that it was common for slaveholders to sell slave-children from their families; however, the typical age at which they were sold is the subject of much debate. As mentioned previously, Frederic Bancroft found that mothers and their very young children were often exempt from separation. Fogel and Engerman maintained that only 9.3% of the New Orleans sales were of children under the age of thirteen.[38] They seem to have adopted the contention of Ulrich B. Phillips that young children were hardly ever sold separately and the view that slaveholders sold slave-children at ages when it would have been normal for them to have left their families.[39]

We can only speculate as to what Fogel and Engerman meant by "normal." Arguably, we might find it normal for a child to leave his family when he is emotionally secure enough to set out on his own. We might understand the normal circumstances under which a slaveholder's child of the age of thirteen or fourteen would have left his family of his own free will and after having consulted with his parents, but we cannot say the same of the slave-child. Neither he nor his parents were empowered to make decisions concerning his psychological or emotional preparedness for separation.

Given the economic rationale for selling his slaves, the slaveholder's most important consideration in determining to sell a slave-child would have been that child's salability. If he were convinced he would profit from the sale, the master would have sold that child. The owner of Louis Hughes, for example, sold him away from his mother at the young age of six—hardly an age when a child would have reached emotional maturity. Mary Reynolds was just about big enough to start playing with a broom and sweeping up—not even half doing that—when her master sold her.[40] Jane Simpson was sold six times in her life—three times before she reached the age of ten.[41]

Samuel Ringgold Ward understood the calculating nature of the slaveholder and the criteria he applied in deciding when his young slave-child was ready for the auction block. He wrote,

However, this sickly boy, if practicable, must be raised for the auction mart. Now to sell his mother immediately, depriving him of her tender care, might endanger his life, and what was all-important in his life, his *salability* . . . . Who knows but, judging from this pedigree, it may prove to be a prime lot— rising six feet in length, and weighing two-hundred and twenty pounds, more or less, some day . . . . Therefore the sale was delayed; the young animal was to run awhile longer . . . .[42]

According to Frederic Bancroft, as a rule there was a dividing line between slave-children who were worth more with their mothers and those who were worth more without them. He drew that line at about eight years of age.[43] Bancroft cited the high prices small slave-children commanded on the auction block as evidence that their sales were very numerous.[44] Fogel and Engerman argued that the selling singly of slave-children under the age of thirteen was infrequent, but Bancroft found that virtually all slave traders sold slave-children from ten to twelve years of age, and many slave traders advertised for those as young as six years of age.[45] We know that the slave trader George Kephert placed an advertisement in the *Alexandria Gazette*, indicating that he was willing to offer the highest cash price for black slaves from ten to twenty-five years of age.[46] Matthew Bliss & Co., a slave-trading company, advertised a bondswoman twenty-four years of age and her two children, one eight and the other three years old. It is noteworthy that the company advised in the ad that the mother and her children "will be sold *separately* or together, *as desired.*"[47]

At nine years of age Thomas H. Jones was snatched away from his only home and his sister Sarah was sold soon after. Jones said that his "poor mother never looked up after this final act of cruelty was accomplished."[48] Moses Grandy remembered four sisters and four brothers; his mother had more children but they were dead or sold away before he could remember them.[49] Sojourner Truth, the second youngest child in her family, did not know the exact number of her siblings because her owner sold away all her older brothers and sisters before she was old enough to remember them. She wrote, however, that the two that immediately preceded her, a five-year-old boy and a three-year-old girl, were sold away when she was an infant.[50]

Conclusion

In writing about the break-up of slave families, most American historians depict humane home-breakers. They insist that moral, not only economic, factors weighed in on the slaveholder's decision to separate slave family members, but the master's public relations strategy was merely to project the appearance of being humane. During the ante-bellum period, thousands of slaves—particularly from east coastal states such as Maryland and Virginia—were exported annually to other slaveholding states. The thick traffic in slave-trading during that period belies the claim that slaveholders agonized over separating slave family members. Indeed, the notion that the typical master was burdened by conscience is a fallacy.

When slaveholders encouraged their slaves to pair up, it was generally to create slave labor, discourage runaways, and maintain discipline. Semi-clad slave-women, forced to mate with men of their owners' choosing, were unfairly labeled sexually promiscuous. But those slaves who voluntarily took on partners understood the value of monogamous unions in helping them to cope with the dehumanizing effects of the American slavery regime. A desire for profit, however, precluded many slaveholders from respecting those unions. The break-up of slave marriages was widespread. During the ante-bellum period, slave sales probably were responsible for forcibly dissolving between 25% and 33% of all slave unions. First and foremost, slave marital arrangements had to satisfy the master's economic needs, and such bonds existed only so long as they served those needs. For the many slave-couples who were split up through sale, the consequences were emotionally devastating. Certain slaveholders encouraged slaves to take on new companions and others compelled them to do it, but there was no more of a guarantee that the new relationship might not be dissolved by another sale.

Slaveholders were not averse to selling young slave-children from their families. Even slave-babies were snatched from their mothers' breasts and sold away to traders. A slave-child eight years of age or older was probably worth more on the auction block without his mother. If convinced of profiting from the sale, the master would have sold that child. It was the money—the slave-child's salability—not his emotional preparedness for separation that mattered. Driven purely by their material interests, many slaveholders thought that Africans in America had no right to any family ties of their own. Countless black people died heartbroken because of it.

Notes

1. Frederic Bancroft, *Slave Trading in the Old South* (Baltimore, Md.: J. H. Furst Company, 1931; reprinted, New York: Fredrick Unger Publishing Company, 1959), 19.

2. Allan Kulikoff, "The Origins of Afro-American Society in Tidewater, Maryland and Virginia, 1700-1790," in *William and Mary Quarterly,* 3rd Series, vol. 35, no. 2 (April 1978): 229.

3. Bancroft, *Slave Trading in the Old South,* 69.

4. Bancroft, *Slave Trading in the Old South,* 53.

5. William Calderhead, "How Extensive Was the Border State Slave Trade? A New Look," *Civil War History,* XVIII (March 1972): 43.

6. Maryland's slave population decreased from 102,994 to 89,737. *Statistics of the Population of the United States, Embracing the Tables of Race, Nationality, Sex, Selected Ages and Occupations . . . Compiled from the Original Returns of the Ninth Census (June 1, 1870)* (Wash., D.C.: U.S. Government Printing Office, 1872), 7.

7. *Statistics of the Population of the United States,* 36-37.

8. The counties were Anne Arundel, Prince George's, Kent, Talbot, Harford, Carroll, Baltimore, and Howard. Calderhead, "How Extensive Was the Border State Slave Trade?" 51.

9. Calderhead, "How Extensive Was the Border State Slave Trade?" 51.

10. Herbert G. Gutman, *Slavery and the Numbers Game* (Chicago: University of Illinois Press, 1975), 137-38.

11. The Virginia slave population decreased from 469,757 to 448,987. *Statistics of the Population of the United States,* 7.

12. Kenneth M. Stampp, *The Peculiar Institution: Slavery in the Ante-Bellum South* (New York: Vintage Books, 1956), 238.

13. Thomas R. Dew, *Review of the Debate of the Virginia Legislature of 1831 and 1832* (Richmond: T. W. White, 1832), 357, 359. Also see *The Pro-Slavery Argument as Maintained by the Most Distinguished Writers of the Southern States* (Charleston: Walker, Richards and Company, 1852), 287-490. Thomas R. Dew was born in 1802 in Tidewater, Virginia to a plantation owning family. He later became a teacher, lawyer, philosopher, and a forerunner of pro-slavery writing.

14. The Virginia slave population in 1830 was 469,757 and Bancroft estimated that a natural increase of 24.2% would have brought that figure to 583,438 by 1840. Allowing for emancipations and successful runaways, he concluded that exportations for the decade were 117,938 or approximately 11,800 per year. Bancroft, *Slave Trading in the Old South*, 384-85.

15. Georgia's slave population increased from 217,531 to 280,944, Tennessee's slave population increased from 141,603 to 183,059, Louisiana's slave population increased from 109,588 to 168,452, Alabama's slave population increased from 117,549 to 253,532, Missouri's slave population grew from 25,091 to 58,240, Mississippi's increased from 65,659 to 195,211, and the Arkansas slave population grew from 4,576 to 19,935. *Statistics of the Population of the United States*, 7.

16. Charles H. Nichols, *Many Thousand Gone: The Ex-Slaves' Account of Their Bondage and Freedom* (Leiden, Netherlands: E. J. Brill, 1963), 20.

17. For example, Fogel and Engerman maintained that the "total interregional sales of children amounted to 234 per annum." Robert W. Fogel and Stanley L. Engerman, *Time on the Cross*, (Boston: Little, Brown & Co., 1974), 48-49.

18. Herbert G. Gutman, *The Black Family in Slavery and Freedom* (New York: Vintage Books, 1977), 75.

19. Peter Kolchin, *American Slavery 1619-1877* (New York: Hill and Wang, 1993), 125-26.

20. William Goodell, *The American Slave Code in Theory and Practice: Its Distinctive Features Shown by Its Statutes, Judicial Decisions, and Illustrative Facts* (New York: American and Foreign Anti-Slavery Society, 1853), part 1, ch. 8, 117; taken from Rev. Theodore D. Weld et al, ed., *Slavery as It Is: Testimony of a Thousand Witnesses* (New York: American Anti-Slavery Society, 1839), 56-57.

21. Charles Ball, *Slavery in the United States: A Narrative of the Life and Adventures of Charles Ball, a Black Man, Who Lived Forty Years in Maryland, South Carolina and Georgia, as a Slave* (Lewistown, Pa.: J. W. Shugert, 1836), 10-12.

22. Lunsford Lane, *The Narrative of Lunsford Lane, Formerly of Raleigh, N.C. Embracing an Account of his Early Life, the Redemption by Purchase of Himself and Family from Slavery*, 4th ed. (Boston: Printed for the publisher. Hewes and Watson's Print, 1848), 19.

23. *Born in Slavery: Slave Narratives from the Federal Writers' Project, 1936-1938* (Wash., D.C.: Library of Congress, 2001), Indiana Narratives, vol. 5, 29. <memory.loc.gov/ammem/snhtml/snhome> (15 April 2006).

24. *Born in Slavery: Slave Narratives from the Federal Writers' Project*, South Carolina Narratives, vol. 11, 31.

25. Jacques Maquet, *Africanity: The Cultural Unity of Black Africa* (New York: Oxford University Press, 1972), 56.For more on the extended family, see Herbert G. Gutman's *The Black Family in Slavery and Freedom 1750-1925* (New York: Vintage Books, 1977); Eric O. Ayisi's *Introduction to the Study of African Culture* (London:

Heinemann Educational Books Ltd., 1972), 16; and Cheikh Anta Diop's *The Cultural Unity of Black Africa* (Chicago: Third World Press, 1978).

26. Norman Y. Yetman, ed., *Voices from Slavery: 100 Authentic Slave Narratives* (Toronto: General Publishing Company, Ltd., 2000), 133.

27. Moses Grandy, *Narrative of the Life of Moses Grandy, Late a Slave in the United States of America* (Boston: O. Johnson Publishing Company, 1844), 31.

28. James L. Smith, *Autobiography of James L. Smith* (Norwich, Connecticut: Press of the Bulletin Company, 1881), 13.

29. Harriet Brent Jacobs, *Incidents in the Life of a Slave Girl*, ed. L. Maria Child (Boston: Acts of Congress, 1861), 26-27.

30. Bancroft, *Slave Trading in the Old South*, 208.

31. Grandy, *Narrative of the Life of Moses Grandy*, 36.

32. William Wells Brown, *Narrative of William Wells Brown* (Boston, 1847), 26.

33. Bancroft, *Slave Trading in the Old South*, 200. Bancroft cited McDougle, "Slavery in Kentucky" *Journal of Negro History* 3, 234-35, who reported the results of sales of forty-six slaves of both sexes and all ages. All but ten slaves were sold in settlement of estates of deceased masters. All but one mother with children six months, four years and six years old respectively were sold singly.

34. Bancroft, *Slave Trading in the Old South*, 199.

35. *Born in Slavery: Slave Narratives from the Federal Writers' Project*, Georgia Narratives, vol. 4, part 1, 168.

36. John W. Blassingame, ed., *Slave Testimony* (Baton Rouge: Louisiana State University Press, 1977), 160.

37. Blassingame, *Slave Testimony*, 269.

38. Fogel and Engerman, *Time on the Cross*, 49.

39. Ulrich B. Phillips, *American Negro Slavery: A Survey of the Supply, Employment and Control of Negro Labor as Determined by the Plantation Regime* (1918; reprinted Baton Rouge: Louisiana State University Press, 1989), 369.

40. *Born in Slavery: Slave Narratives from the Federal Writers' Project, 1936-1938*, Texas Narratives, vol. 16, part 3, 237.

41. *Born in Slavery: Slave Narratives from the Federal Writers' Project, 1936-1938*, Missouri Narratives, vol.10, 311-12.

42. Samuel Ringgold Ward, *Autobiography of a Fugitive Negro: His Anti-Slavery Labours in the United States, Canada & England* (1855; reprinted New York: Arno Press and the New York Times, 1968), 17-19.

43. Bancroft, *Slave Trading in the Old South*, 197.

44. Bancroft, *Slave Trading in the Old South*, 208.

45. Bancroft, *Slave Trading in the Old South*, 208.

46. Goodell, *The American Slave Code*, part 1, ch. 2, 54.

47. Goodell, *The American Slave Code*, part 1, ch. 2, 54.

48. Thomas H. Jones, *The Experiences of Thomas H. Jones, Who was a Slave for Forty-Three Years* (Boston: Boyin and Chandler, 37 Cornhill, 1862), 8-9.

49. Grandy, *Narrative of the Life of Moses Grandy*, 5.

50. Sojourner Truth, *Narrative of Sojourner Truth* (New York: Arno Press and the New York Times, 1968), 15.

PART FOUR

The Aftermath

CHAPTER NINETEEN

One Hundred More Years of Racism and Cruelty

They've lynched a man in Dixie.
O God, behold the crime.
And midst the mad mob's howling
How sweet the church bells chime!
They've lynch a man in Dixie.
You say this cannot be?
See where his lead-torn body
Mute hangs from yonder tree.

—JOSHUA HENRY JONES,
The Heart of the World, 1919

Scholars debate whether permanent psychological scars were inflicted upon black people by American slavery or they emerged from its brutality relatively unscathed. As mentioned previously, the historian Stanley Elkins argued that the heritage of American slavery forever crippled black people. He charged it responsible for the psychological, social, economic, and political condition of blacks in the 1950s. Even today, a black psychologist and two black licensed clinical social workers have coined the phrase "post traumatic slavery disorder."[1] They contend that current dysfunctional behaviors and disorders that exist among black people have origins linked to American slavery, and they suggest that there is an intergenerational transmission of the slavery trauma.[2]

Their argument, however, does not have the ring of truth—primarily because American slavery was legally abolished over 145 years ago. Another more rational explanation exists for rejecting the contention that the heritage of American slavery psychologically crippled black people. Any discussion of American slavery and its lasting effect, if any, on African-Americans today must consider that neither President Abraham Lincoln's Emancipation Proclamation of January 1, 1863 nor the Thirteenth and Fourteenth Amendments to the United States Constitution abated the coercive, psychological, social, economic, and political manifestations of racism practiced by whites. The ideology of white supremacy, which underpinned the American slavery regime, did not die with American slavery; it survived well into the twentieth century. Black people emerged from the horrors of slavery only to face post-bellum and twentieth-century forms of racism and savagery.

Indeed, the hundred years immediately following the period of American slavery was a brutal and fearful period for black people. After the Civil War, the Ku Klux Klan and Southern and border-state police forces replaced the slave patrols in terrorizing Southern blacks and maintaining the social order.[3] Mindful that black men were no longer their valuable personal property, Southern whites began murdering them at an alarming rate. While the white Southerner's gun remained, his rope, his match, and his gasoline replaced his bullwhip as his favored implements of death. The historian Robert A. Gibson wrote, "In the last decades of the nineteenth century, the lynching of black people in the Southern and border-states became an institutionalized method used by whites to terrorize blacks and maintain white supremacy."[4] Generally defined as a public and spontaneous extrajudicial killing by mob action, lynching was the violent means by which white Southerners maintained control over black Southerners. Although most killings consisted of hangings and shootings, more ghastly forms included maiming and dismemberment, castration, and burning at the stake.[5]

From the last two decades of the nineteenth century through the first half of the twentieth century, it is estimated that from 2,800 to nearly 5,000 murders by lynching occurred in America. Black people constituted roughly 73% of the victims.[6] Ninety percent of all lynching occurred in the Southern states, but of the remaining 10%, one-third took place in Southern border-states.[7] The state of Mississippi led the nation with the highest incidence of lynching, closely followed by the states of Georgia and Texas.[8] In 1892, the number of killings by lynching reached its peak; that year, an estimated 161 blacks and 69 whites were lynched.[9]

While the turn of the century marked a gradual decline in the number of murders by lynching, the number of deaths accompanied by fiendish methods of torture such as the dismemberment of fingers and ears, the boring of corkscrews in the flesh, and the burning alive of bodies became increasingly frequent. Public indifference to this unbelievable torture grew as well.[10] Consequently, the federal government relinquished its constitutional responsibility to protect the lives of Southern blacks when neither Congress nor the executive branch of the United States Government took action to prevent lynching. State law enforcement officials looked the other way and refused to prosecute the perpetrators—even when those officials had advance notice of the lynching event.[11]

During the post-Reconstruction period, the imagery of black men raping white women in the South arose as a purely political invention—a pretext for terrorizing Southern blacks. Ante-bellum-era Southern whites generally did not label black bondsmen rapists, and we know that throughout the Civil War (when thousands of Southern white men were away fighting the Union over the issue of whether or not slavery in the South would spread to other territories annexed by the United States) not one black man in the South was charged with raping a white woman.[12] But as a justification for the practice of lynching, post-Reconstruction-era white Southerners assuredly offered the popular racist myth that black men harbored uncontrollable, animal-like impulses to rape white women and their daughters.[13] In one instance in a speech delivered to the Georgia Agricultural Society at its annual meeting on August 11, 1897, Rebecca Latimer Felton, a crusader for white women's rights, may have convinced her audience that black rapists were the greatest threat facing poor white women. "If it needs lynching to protect woman's dearest possession from the ravening human beasts," Felton declared, "then I say lynch, a thousand times a week if necessary."[14] Ironically, from the years 1882 to 1927, white Southerners lynched an estimated seventy-six black women.[15] It is unlikely that those black women were murdered for raping white women or their daughters.

The white Southerner's insistence that his woman's virtue required protection from black rapists was racist demagoguery—employed as an excuse to subjugate black Southerners and dissuade them from pursuing economic self-sufficiency. In fact, Southern whites made allegations of murder and of felonious assault most frequently as their justification for lynching black people.[16]

Black women, most notably the journalist and lecturer Ida B. Wells (1862-1931), were at the forefront of the anti-lynching crusade. For decades, they courageously spoke out against the lynching of law-abiding black men. In her weekly newspaper, *Memphis Free Speech*, Wells printed the following editorial on May 21, 1892, condemning the use of the fraudulent rape charge as a pretext for murdering black men:

> Eight Negroes lynched since last issue of the *Free Speech*, one at Little Rock, Ark., last Saturday morning where citizens broke into the penitentiary and got their man; three near Anniston, Ala., one near New Orleans; three at Clarksville, Ga., the last three for killing a white man, and five on the same old racket—the new alarm about raping white women. The same program of hanging, then shooting bullets into the lifeless bodies was carried out to the letter. Nobody in this section of the country believes the old threadbare lie that Negro men rape white women. If Southern white men are not careful, they will overreach themselves and public sentiment will have a reaction; a conclusion will then be reached which will be very damaging to the moral reputation of their women.[17]

As a consequence of printing the editorial, her newspaper's office was ransacked and her property destroyed. Undeterred, Wells became an exile from Memphis, Tennessee and continued to give lectures in the United States and England about the evils of lynching. She organized anti-lynching societies as well and published pamphlets documenting the South's disturbing lynching record.[18]

In 1904, Mary Church Terrell (1863-1954), the honorary president of the National Association of Colored Women, published an article in the *North American Review* entitled "Lynching from a Negro's Point of View." In that article, she urged ministers and good Christians to protest against what she called a "rising tide of barbarism which threatens to deluge the whole land."[19]

The Emancipation Proclamation and black advancement during Reconstruction, some real and some merely perceived, helped to remove the stigma of black servitude and change Southern whites' perception of their own social, economic, and political standing vis-à-vis that of Southern blacks. Nonetheless, the average white Southerner held on stubbornly to his three major stereotypical images of blacks: the menial who knew how to stay in his place, the shiftless happy-go-lucky buffoon, and what Walter White called "the habitual criminal of unrestrained appetites."[20] From the post-Reconstruction period through the early twentieth century, Southern whites attempted to convince the rest of the country that the lynching of blacks was necessary to deter rape and other criminal activity. The North Carolina ex-slave W. L. Post and other blacks who lived through the period knew better. Post understood that the white Southerner lynched the black man who tried "to get nervy or to have a little bit for himself."[21] In other words, white Southerners lynched black people to enforce docility in the black community, maintain the social order, and discourage black economic advancement.

Stereotypes aside, Southern whites feared not only black social and economic progress; they feared losing black labor as well.[22] The control of exploited black labor was a major impetus behind the development of modern police forces in Atlanta, Charleston, and New Orleans.[23] Indeed, hundreds of thousands of free black men were arrested, charged with and convicted of violating anti-vagrancy and other laws, and under the convict leasing system, leased to forced labor camps owned and operated by white Southerners.[24] Moreover, Jim Crow laws relegated Southern blacks to performing cheap labor as sharecroppers on farms controlled by their former captors.[25] White police forces throughout the South were bound to dutifully enforce those laws when they were violated by blacks. When white mobs attacked black people, those blacks received no protection from the police; some officers stood by, others participated in the attacks.[26]

As Danu Smith explains, Southern white police repression continued throughout the civil rights era:

> During the Civil Rights Movement, the world watched in horror and shock as white policemen with their horses, clubs and dogs, savagely beat and arrested blacks for demonstrating against Jim Crow. Throughout the 60's when blacks violently rebelled in many urban areas against oppressive conditions, the po-

lice and National Guard wantonly killed a number of participants and conducted sweeping mass arrests. . . . Police repression is and has been historically, a matter of official policy often sanctioned and encouraged at the highest level of our government.[27]

During the decade of the 1960s, police killed black men at a rate some nine-to-thirteen times higher than they killed white men. Between 1968 and 1969, for instance, police officers in the United States killed 1,188 black males and 1,253 white males in a population of which only about 10% were black.[28] They killed blacks at a rate that was consistently nine times as high as that of whites over an eighteen-year period.[29]

Just as black folk during the last decade of the nineteenth century and early twentieth century were angered by, but powerless to stop, white Southerners who increasingly lynched their people, today there is perhaps no issue as volatile in the black community as police extrajudicial use of deadly force. Currently, most police shootings occur at night in urban ghetto areas and involve white patrol officers and male civilians of color between the ages of nineteen and twenty-nine. Because law enforcement officers prefer adhering to a blue code of silence rather than exposing the criminal conduct of their brethren, police in every region of the United States continue to unjustly target young black men as "suspected criminals," kill them, and serve no prison time.[30] In fact, white police officers in America are rarely convicted of murdering young black men.

The historian Stanley Elkins accused black people of infantilism. He ascribed it to the survival of a slave mentality. He was wrong. The American slavery experience—as horrifying as it was—did not forever cripple black people psychologically or turn them into a group of abnormally dependent children. Post-Reconstruction, twentieth-century, and present-day forms of white violence, repression, and racial discrimination have hindered and continue to impede black social and economic advancement.

Notes

1. Omar G. Reid, Sekou Mims and Larry Higginbottom, *Post Traumatic Slavery Disorder* (Charlotte, N.C.: Conquering Books, LLC, 2004).

2. Reid, *Post Traumatic Slavery Disorder,* 10.

3. Danu Smith, "The Upsurge of Police Repression: An Analysis," *Black Scholar* 12, no. 1 (January/February 1981): 38. In 1866, former Confederate General Nathan Bedford Forrest founded the first Ku Klux Klan in the town of Pulaski, Tennessee to fight the governments of Reconstruction and maintain the existing social order through racial terror.

4. Robert A. Gibson, "The Negro Holocaust: Lynching and Race Riots in the United States, 1880-1950" *Yale-New Haven Teachers Institute* (1979): 2. <http://www.yale.edu/ynhti/curriculum/units/1979/2/79.02.07.x.html> (29 Feb. 2007)

5. Gibson, "The Negro Holocaust," 2.

6. In 1919, the National Association for the Advancement of Colored People reported 3,386 incidents of lynching between 1882 and 1918, 2,522 of which were blacks. *Thirty Years of Lynching In The United States: 1889-1918* (New York: National Association for the Advancement of Colored People, 1919), 29. Walter White reported that 4,951 persons were lynched between 1882 and 1927. Of that number, 1,438 were white and 3,513 were black. Walter White, *Rope and Faggot: A Biography of Judge Lynch* (New York: Alfred A. Knopf, Inc., 1926; reprinted Notre Dame, Indiana: University of Notre Dame Press, 2001), 267. The Tuskegee Institute statistics show that between the years 1882 and 1951, 4,730 people were lynched in the United States: 3,437 blacks and 1,293 whites. Jessie Parkhurst Guzman, ed., *1952 Negro Yearbook* (New York: William H. Wise, 1952), 275-79. The sociologists Stewart E. Tolnay and E. M. Beck found that only 2,805 killings by lynching are documented between 1882 and 1930, of which 2,462 victims were black. Stewart E. Tolnay and E. M. Beck, *A Festival of Violence: An Analysis of Southern Lynchings, 1882-1930* (Urbana and Chicago: University of Illinois Press, 1995), 269.

7. Mary Frances Berry, *Black Resistance White Law: A History of Constitutional Racism in America* (New York: Allen Lane The Penguin Press, 1994), 98; Gunnar Myrdal, *An American Dilemma* (New York: Harper & Brothers, 1944), 560-61.

8. Myrdal, *An American Dilemma*, 560-61. Between the years 1882 and 1927, the state of Mississippi had an estimated 561 killings by lynching: 44 whites and 517 blacks. The states of Georgia and Texas had an estimated 549 and 534 murders by lynching respectively. White, *Rope and Faggot*, 255-58.

9. Gibson, "The Negro Holocaust," 2.

10. White, *Rope and Faggot*, 33-38.

11. Berry, *Black Resistance White Law*, 98.

12. Angela Y. Davis, *Women, Race & Class* (New York: Vintage Books,1983), 184.

13. For more on the myth of the black rapist see, Davis, *Women, Race & Class*, 173-84.

14. Jerome A. McDuffe, *Politics in Wilmington and New Hanover County, North Carolina, 1865-1900: The Genesis of a Race Riot*, 2 vols. (Ph.D. diss., Kent State University, 1979) <www.1989wilmingon.com/AlexanderManlyRebeccaFelton> (12 Feb. 2006).

15. White, *Rope and Faggot*, 267.

16. Gibson wrote, "The accusations against persons lynched, according to the Tuskegee Institute records for the years 1882 to 1951, were: in 41% for felonious assault, 19.2% for rape, 6.1% for attempted rape, 4.9% for robbery and theft, 1.8% for insult to white persons, and 22.7% for miscellaneous offenses or no offense at a 11.5%." Gibson, "The Negro Holocaust," 3. James Elbert Cutler found that of the 2,060 blacks lynched between the years 1882 and 1903 only 707 blacks or 34.3% were charged with "the crime of rape, either attempted, alleged or actually committed." James Elbert Cutler, *Lynch-Law* (New York: Longmans, Green & Co., 1905), 178. Walter White, relying on statistics published by the National Association for the Advancement of Colored People, found that of the 2,522 blacks murdered by lynching between 1889 and 1918, the greatest possible total of blacks "charged with rape, alleged rape, attempted rape, suspicion of rape, or of offences of any other nature, no matter how slight, against white women" is 714 or 28.3%. White, *Rope and Faggot*, 253.

17. Ida B. Wells-Barnett, *On Lynchings* (New York: Humanity Books, 2002), 61.

18. Wells-Barnett, *On Lynchings*, 5.

19. Mary Church Terrell, "Lynching from a Negro's Point of View," *North American Review* 178 (1904): 853-68.

20. White, *Rope and Faggot*, 10.

21. Norman Y. Yetman, ed., *Voices from Slavery: 100 Authentic Slave Narratives* (Toronto: General Publishing Company, Ltd., 2000), 38.

22. White, *Rope and Faggot*, 96-97.

23. Susie Bernstein, Lynn Cooper et al., *The Iron Fist and the Velvet Glove, An Analysis of U.S. Police* (Berkeley, California: The Center for Research On Criminal Justice, 1977), 29.

24. Douglas A. Blackmon, *Slavery by Another Name: The Re-Enslavement of Black Americans from the Civil War to World War II* (New York: Doubleday, 2008), p. 7.

25. Claud Anderson, Ed.D, *Black Labor, White Wealth: The Search for Power and Economic Justice* (Edgewood, Md.: Duncan & Duncan, Inc., 1994), 161.

26. Danu Smith, "The Upsurge of Police Repression: An Analysis," in *Black Scholar* 12, no. 1 (January/February 1981): 38.

27. Smith, "The Upsurge of Police Repression," 38.

28. Paul Takagi, "Death By 'Police Intervention'," in *A Community Concern: Police Use of Deadly Force*, ed. Robert N. Brenner and Marjorie Kravitz (Washington: U.S. Dept. of Justice, Law Enforcement Assistance Administration, National Institute of Law Enforcement and Criminal Justice, January 1979), 33.

29. Lennox S. Hinds, "The Police Use of Excessive and Deadly Force: Racial Implications," in *A Community Concern: Police Use of Deadly Force*, ed. Robert N. Brenner and Marjorie Kravitz (Washington: U.S. Dept. of Justice, Law Enforcement Assistance Administration, National Institute of Law Enforcement and Criminal Justice, January 1979), 8.

30. On September 8, 1994, black nineteen-year-old Daryl Howerton was shot six times and killed by Greensboro, North Carolina police officers Charles Fletcher and Jose Blanco after they had been called by a witness to come and take him to a hospital. On September 21, 1996, off-duty white Detroit police officer Eugene Brown shot unarmed black twenty-year-old Lamar Grable multiple times in the chest at point blank range, killing him. On April 14, 1997, white East Haven police officer Robert Flodquist gunned down black twenty-one-year-old Malik Jones in New Haven, Connecticut after chasing him from East Haven because of a report that he was driving erratically. On February 4, 1999, four white New York City police officers fired 41 shots at unarmed West African immigrant Amadou Diallo, striking him 19 times and killing him as he stood in the vestibule of his apartment building. On April 11, 1999, an innocent twenty-seven-year-old black man, Earl Faison, was wrongly apprehended as a suspect in the murder of a police officer and died after being in Orange, New Jersey police custody for 45 minutes. On May 13, 1999, unarmed black eighteen-year-old Desmond Rudolph was shot at 22 times and killed by white Louisville, Kentucky police officers Chris Horn and Paul Kincade. Rudolph was hit at least ten times—six bullets entering his head. Black nineteen-year-old Timothy Thomas was fatally shot by white Cincinnati, Ohio police officer Stephen Roach on April 7, 2001 after being pursued on outstanding traffic violation warrants. Since 1995, at least eighteen black males have died at the hands of Cincinnati police. On May 18, 2001, black twenty-two-year-old High Point, North Carolina resident Gil Barber was shot to death by white Guilford County Deputy Sheriff Thomas Gordy after Barber was injured in a one-car accident. Barber was unarmed, not wanted for any crime, and not under the influence of alcohol or

drugs. On May 17, 2003, black Richmond, Virginia police detective David D. Melvin fatally shot unarmed black twenty-nine-year-old robbery suspect Verlon M. Johnson in the heart with a .357 handgun, while he stood bare-chested on his front porch with a toothbrush in his mouth. On July 5, 2003, Asian-American Denver, Colorado police officer James Turney shot and killed black fifteen-year-old developmentally disabled Paul Childs during a domestic dispute. Officer Turney was also the key shooter in the January 30, 2002 death of black eighteen-year-old hearing-impaired Gregory Smith. On February 2, 2002, off-duty San Francisco police officer Steve Lee shot unarmed thirty-seven-year-old black street vendor Gregory Hooper four times in the chest at point-blank range, killing him. On November 30, 2003, unarmed black forty-one-year-old Nathaniel Jones died after two white Cincinnati police officers clubbed him at least a dozen times. On December 10, 2003, unarmed black thirty-nine-year-old Kenneth B. Walker was riding in a GMC Yukon truck with three friends in Columbus, Georgia when, suspected of carrying guns and drugs, he was pulled over on Interstate 185 by members of the Muscogee County Sheriff's Department and ordered to exit the vehicle. White Muscogee County Deputy Sheriff David Glisson shot him in the head, killing him. No guns or drugs were found in the SUV. On January 3, 2004, white Louisville, Kentucky undercover police officer McKenzie Mattingly shot black nineteen-year-old Michael Newby three times in the back as he ran, killing him. Newby was the seventh black man killed by Louisville police since 1998. On May 5, 2004, San Francisco undercover police officers gunned down unarmed black disabled young Cammerin Boyd while his hands were raised in the air surrendering. On May 7, 2005, without justification, white Hartford, Connecticut police officer Robert Lawlor fired three shots striking unarmed black eighteen-year-old Jashon Bryant from behind and killing him as he sat in the passenger seat of a car that his friend was driving away. On September 4, 2005, New Orleans Police Officers shot and killed black unarmed forty-year-old mentally retarded Ronald Madison as he was crossing a bridge on his way to his brother's dental office. The coroner said that Mr. Madison was shot seven times in total, with five wounds in his back. The police officers were hailed as heroes by their fellow officers, the district attorney did not seek the death penalty, and all except one of the officers are still on the job. On January 6, 2006, seven guards of the Bay County Sheriff's Office Boot Camp in Florida, Lt. Charles Helms Jr., Raymond   Hauck,   Henry McFadden, Joseph Walsh II, Charles Enfinger, Patrick Garrett, and Henry Dickens, were caught on video tape viciously beating and suffocating unarmed black fourteen-year-old Martin Lee Anderson to death while a nurse, Kristin Anne Schmidt, stood by and did nothing. On October 12, 2007, an all-white Bay County jury acquitted all eight perpetrators of charges of aggravated manslaughter of a child, child neglect, and culpable negligence. On November 25, 2006, five NYPD undercover officers unloaded fifty rounds at twenty-three-year-old unarmed black groom Sean Bell's grey Nissan Altima as he and his two unarmed friends drove away from his bachelor party in Queens, New York. The NYPD officers struck Bell three times, killing him just hours before his wedding. White NYPD Detective Michael Oliver fired thirty-one of the fifty shots. Although three detectives, Michael Oliver, Gescard Isnora, and Marc Cooper, were charged with counts varying from manslaughter to reckless endangerment in the slaying, after a bench trial Queens Supreme Court Justice Arthur Cooperman acquitted all three of all charges on April 25, 2008. On November 12, 2007, five NYPD police officers fired a hail of twenty bullets, hitting black eighteen-year-old unarmed mentally-ill Khiel Coppin eight times and killing him. The officers claimed that Mr. Coppin was about to use deadly force; however, he had been holding only a black hair brush.

CHAPTER TWENTY

Epilogue

My purpose in writing this book was to reveal the full horrors of ante-bellum-era American slavery by allowing those courageous former slaves who actually suffered through it to tell us their stories. It was to expose facts about American slavery rarely found in most history books on the subject. The disturbing facts contained in this book will probably give little comfort to the majority of Americans. Nonetheless, for the sake of fully educating the public about American slavery, I felt compelled to offer my contribution to what is, in my view, an incomplete record of a dark period in our history. Inevitably, certain people will ask, "Why expose us to such a violent and horrific past?" Others might ask, "Who really wants to read about American slavery?" Still others will ask, "Are you looking for reparations?" I believe that we should be educated about our country's shameful past in order to fully understand it—to understand and then acknowledge that with a monopoly of violence, white people in our country gained an insurmountable economic advantage over black people by forcibly taking and using up their labor and denying them the educational, economic, legal, social, and political rights and privileges white men in America enjoyed.

But mine is not a demand for reparations. My feeling is one of ambivalence about that issue. Mine is a challenge to all to treat all human beings fairly and equally in the important matters that affect their lives, without considerations of race and color. Those matters include equal access to educational, employment, and housing opportunities, as well as fair and impartial justice. It is my wish that after having read this book, we will garner the courage and the resolve to plot a righteous course—to work toward establishing a truly race-neutral American society.

I am fully cognizant of the fact that the present is not the past; today is not yesterday. And today I am guardedly optimistic about the future of race relations in the United States. No doubt, attitudes about race in America have changed for the better over the last thirty years. The Civil Rights Acts of the 1960s marked the beginning of a period devoted to the legal protection of the political, employment, housing, and public accommodation rights of all American citizens. Moreover, our children are in large part responsible and should also be credited for some of the positive change in racial attitudes in our country. Most are better able to understand the importance, and to accept the moral imperative, of racial equality and full inclusion for all Americans.

There are other signs that our country appears to be moving—albeit incrementally—in a positive direction. Evidence of the movement toward racial equality and full inclusion can be seen in the political arena. For example, on November 7, 2006 the citizens of Commonwealth of Massachusetts elected Deval Patrick as their 71st governor, the first black governor elected north of the Mason-Dixon Line, and on November 4, 2008, for the first time in our country's history an African American, Barack Obama, was elected the 44th President of the United States. He believes (as I do) that there is hope for a better future in America.

If, by offering this book, I accomplish the goal of better educating the public about American slavery and helping it to confront a past of which we should not be proud, perhaps embracing a positive future, our country will atone for that past by according all of its citizens the same rights to life, liberty, and the pursuit of happiness to which every human being is entitled—regardless of race, color, sex, religion, sexual preference, and national origin.

Glossary

abolitionist. An individual who advocates ending slavery.

acculturation. The cultural modification of an individual, group, or people by adapting to or borrowing traits from another culture; *also*: a merging of cultures as a result of prolonged contact.

amalgamation. The action or process of two people of different races mixing and merging into a single body.

American Civil War. From April 1861 to April 1865, a civil war in the United States between the North (the Union) and the South (the Confederacy) was fought primarily over the issue of whether slavery in the South would spread to other territories annexed by the United States. More than half a million Americans were killed. The Union victory led to the abolition of slavery throughout the country.

ante-bellum era. The period existing immediately before the Civil War.

broken on the wheel. A form of tortuous execution having been first used in France. The victim is placed on a wagon wheel, his limbs are stretched out along the spokes, the bones of his limbs are broken, and his arms and legs are woven into the spokes of the wheel. The wheel is then mounted atop a pole, with the victim still alive, where he is left to die from exposure.

brogan. A heavy shoe; especially: a coarse work shoe reaching to the ankle.

bullwhip. A rawhide whip with a very long plaited lash.

burn at the stake. To execute a victim by burning his body.

calico. Any of various cheap cotton fabrics with figured patterns.

castration. To deprive of the testes.

chattel. An item of tangible movable or immovable property except real estate and things (as buildings) connected with real property.

concubine. A woman with whom a man cohabits without being married: as a. one having a recognized social status in a household below that of a wife; or b. a woman other than his wife with whom a married man has a continuing sexual relationship.

contubernium. A permitted cohabitation of slaves to which no legal rights were attached.

counter-insurgency. Organized violent activity designed to combat a condition of revolt against a regime. The revolt is less than an organized revolution and not recognized as belligerency.

demographer. One engaged in the statistical study of human populations especially with reference to size and density, distribution, and vital statistics.

dismember. To cut off or disjoin the limbs, members, or parts of a body.

egalitarian. Marked by a belief in human equality especially with respect to social, political, and economic rights and privileges.

Emancipation Proclamation. An executive proclamation, issued on January 1, 1863, by U.S. President Abraham Lincoln, declaring that all persons held in slavery in certain designated states and districts were and should remain free.

Evangelical Protestantism. The result of a broad movement in Protestantism known as the Great Awakening in the eighteenth century and Revivalism in the nineteenth century. The doctrines of Evangelical Protestantism are: that human beings are inherently bad people and must be saved by Christ – thus an emphasis on puritanical morality and rigidity; that personal conversion based on an emotional understanding of one's innate depravity and Christ's redeeming sacrifice is crucial to individual salvation; that converted believers must demonstrate their spirituality by working for others in missionary work, bible societies, anti-slavery movements and other egalitarian social causes; that the converted will be persecuted and such persecution indicates the holiness of the believer, and that every word of the Bible is to be taken literally.

flog. To beat with or as if with a rod, stick, or whip.

Fourteenth Amendment. Ratified in 1868, the Fourteenth Amendment to the U.S. Constitution created or at least recognized for the first time a citizenship of the United States, as distinct from that of the states, forbade the making or enforcement by any state of any law abridging the privileges and immunities of Citizens of the United States, and secured all persons against any state action which resulted in either the deprivation of life, liberty, or property without due process of law, or the denial of the equal protection of the laws.

historiography. The product of historical writing: a body of historical literature.

homicide. The killing of one human being by the act, procurement, or omission of another.

in the family way. Pregnant.

jump over the broom. To get married; a ritual performed by the bride and groom during a slave wedding ceremony.

licentious. Lacking moral restraints; *especially*: disregarding sexual restraints.

manumission. Formal emancipation from slavery.

miscegenation. A mixture of races; *especially*: marriage, cohabitation, or sexual intercourse between a white person and a member of another race.

monogamous. An individual having only one spouse or sex partner.

mutilation. The act of cutting off or permanently destroying a limb or essential part of the body.

overseer. One that supervises; *especially*: one that supervises slaves.

paternalism. A system under which an authority undertakes to supply needs or regulate conduct of those under its control in matters affecting them as individuals as well as in their relations to authority and to each other.

patriarch. A man who is head of a social organization marked by the supremacy of the father in the clan or family, the legal dependence of wives and children, and the reckoning of descent and inheritance in the male line; *broadly*: A man who controls a disproportionately large share of power.

philandering. To have casual or illicit sex with a woman or with many women; *especially*: to be sexually unfaithful to one's wife.

polygamy. The practice of having more than two marriages at the same time.

promiscuity. The indiscriminate selection of persons for sexual intercourse.

slave. A person who is wholly subject to the will of another; one who has no freedom of action, but whose person and services are wholly under the control of another person.

slave codes. Laws which defined the legal relationship between the master and his slave, enacted throughout the South during the late eighteenth and early nineteenth centuries by the slaveholding class.

slave-trade. The traffic in slaves or the buying and selling of slaves for profit.

steal away. To go secretly.

sterilize. To render one incapable of procreation as, for example, tying the female Fallopian tubes or performing a vasectomy.

sudden heat of passion. In the common-law definition of manslaughter, this phrase means an excess of rage or anger, suddenly arising from a contemporaneous provocation. It means that the provocation must arise at the time of the killing, and that the passion is not the result of a former provocation, and the act must be directly caused by the passion arising out of the provocation at the time of the homicide.

Thirteenth Amendment. The Thirteenth Amendment to the U.S. Constitution abolished slavery in the United States in 1865.

toe the mark. To conform rigorously to a rule or standard.

Victorian. Typical of the moral standards, attitudes, or conduct of the age of Alexandrina Victoria, queen of the United Kingdom of Great Britain and Ireland (1837-1901).

WPA Interviews. From 1936 to 1938 during the Depression years, the WPA Federal Writers' Project (FWP) sent out-of-work writers in seventeen states to interview ordinary people in order to write down their life stories. Initially, only four states involved in the project (Virginia, South Carolina, Georgia, and Florida) focused on collecting the stories of ex-slaves. In 1937, John A. Lomax, the National Advisor on Folklore and Folkways for the FWP, directed the remaining states involved in the project to interview former slaves as well. Federal field workers often visited the ex-slaves they interviewed twice in order to gather as many recollections as possible. The workers then turned the narratives over to their state's FWP director for editing and eventual transfer to Washington, D.C.

Bibliography

Akbar, Na'im. "Mental Disorder among African-Americans," *Black Books Bulletin* 7, no. 2 (1981): 18-25.

Anderson, Claud, Ed.D. *Black Labor, White Wealth: The Search for Power and Economic Justice.* Edgewood, Md.: Duncan & Duncan, Inc., 1994.

Aptheker, Herbert. *American Negro Slave Revolts.* New York: International Publishers, 1983.

Ayisi, Eric O. *Introduction to the Study of African Culture.* London: Heinemann Educational Books Ltd., 1972.

Ball, Charles. *Slavery in the United States: A Narrative of the Life and Adventures of Charles Ball, a Black Man, Who Lived Forty Years in Maryland, South Carolina and Georgia, as a Slave.* Lewistown, Pa.: J. W. Shugert, 1836.

Bancroft, Frederic. *Slave Trading in the Old South.* Baltimore, Md., J. H. Furst Company, 1931; reprinted New York: Fredrick Unger Publishing Company, 1959.

Bernstein, Susie and Lynn Cooper et al. *The Iron Fist and the Velvet Glove, An Analysis of U.S. Police.* Berkeley, California: The Center for Research on Criminal Justice, 1977.

Berry, Mary Frances. *Black Resistance White Law: A History of Constitutional Racism in America.* New York: Allen Lane The Penguin Press, 1994.

Bibb, Henry. *Narrative of the Life and Adventures of Henry Bibb, An American Slave.* New York: H. Bibb, 1849.

Blackmon, Douglas A. *Slavery by Another Name: The Re-Enslavement of Black Americans from the Civil War to World War II* New York: Doubleday, 2008.

Blassingame, John W. *The Slave Community: Plantation Life in the Ante-Bellum South.* Rev. and enl. ed. Cary, North Carolina: Oxford University Press, 1979.

------. ed. *Slave Testimony.* Baton Rouge: Louisiana State University Press, 1977.

Born in Slavery: Slave Narratives from the Federal Writers' Project,1936-1938. Wash., D.C.: Library of Congress, 2001.<memory.loc.gov/ammem/snhtml/snhome.html> (15 April 2006).

Brown, John. *Slave Life in Georgia: Narrative of the Life, Sufferings and Escape of John Brown, a Fugitive Slave, Now in England.* London,1855.

Brown, William Wells. *Narrative of William Wells Brown.* Boston, 1847.

Brownmiller, Susan. *Against Our Will.* New York: Bantam Books, 1975.

Burton, Annie L. *Memories of Childhood's Slavery Days.* Boston: Ross Publishing Co., 1909.

Calderhead, William. "How Extensive Was the Border State Slave Trade? A New Look." *Civil War History,* XVIII, (March 1972): 42-55.

Calhoun, Arthur W. *A Social History of the American Family from Colonial Times to the Present.* vol. 2. Cleveland: The Arthur H. Clark Co., 1917.

Cheek, William F. *Black Resistance Before the Civil War.* Beverly Hills, Calif.: Glencoe Press, 1970.

Cooley, Thomas M., LL.D. *The General Principles of Constitutional Law in the United States of America.* Boston: Little Brown & Company, 1898.

Cutler, James Elbert. *Lynch-Law.* New York: Longmans, Green & Co., 1905.

David, Paul A. et al. *Reckoning with Slavery: Critical Essays in the Quantitative History of the American Negro.* New York: Oxford University Press, 1976.

Davis, Angela Y. *Women, Race & Class.* New York: Vintage Books, 1983.

------. "Reflections on the Black Woman's Role in the Community of Slaves," *Black Scholar* 3, no. 4 (December 1971): 1-15.

Davis, David Brion. *Inhuman Bondage: The Rise and Fall of Slavery in the New World.* New York: Oxford University Press, 2006.

De Bow's Review VII (1849).

Dew, Thomas R. *Review of the Debate of the Virginia Legislature of 1831 and 1832* Richmond: T.W. White, 1832.

Diop, Cheikh Anta. *The Cultural Unity of Black Africa.* Chicago: Third World Press, 1978.

Douglass, Frederick. *My Bondage and My Freedom.* Chicago: Johnson Publishing Co., 1970.

------. *Frederick Douglass: The Narrative and Selected Writings.* ed. Michael Meyer. New York: McGraw Hill, 1984.

Elkins, Stanley M. *Slavery: A Problem in American Institutional and Intellectual Life.* Chicago: Univ. of Chicago Press, 1959.

Feldstein, Stanley. *Once A Slave.* New York: William Morrow Company, Inc., 1971.

Felton, Rebecca Latimer. *Country Life in Georgia in the Days of My Youth: Electronic Edition.* Atlanta, Georgia: Index Printing Company, 1919. <docsouth.unc.edu/felton> (12 Feb. 2006).

Ferrall, Simon Ansley. *A Ramble of Six Thousand Miles through the United States of America.* London: E. Wilson, Publisher, 1832.

Fogel, Robert W. and Stanley L. Engerman. *Time on the Cross.* Boston: Little, Brown & Co., 1974.

Franklin, John Hope and Alfred A. Moss, Jr. *From Slavery to Freedom,* 6th ed. New York: Alfred A. Knopf, Inc., 1988.

Frazier, E. Franklin. *The Negro Family in the United States.* Chicago: University of Chicago Press, 1939.

------. *Black Bourgeoisie.* New York: Collier Books, 1962.

French, Mrs. A. M. *Slavery in South Carolina and the Ex-slaves; or, The Port Royal Mission.* New York: Winchell M. French, 1862; reprinted New York: Negro Universities Press, 1969.

Genovese, Eugene D. *Roll Jordan Roll: The World the Slaves Made.* New York: Vintage Books, 1972.

------. *From Rebellion to Revolution.* New York: Vintage Books, 1979.

Gibson, Robert A. "The Negro Holocaust: Lynching and Race Riots in the United States, 1880-1950." *Yale-New Haven Teachers Institute* (1979). <http://www.yale.edu/ynhti/curriculum/units/1979/2/79.02.07.x.html> (29 Feb. 2008)

Goodell, Reverend William. *The American Slave Code in Theory and Practice: Its Distinctive Features Shown by Its Statutes, Judicial Decisions, and Illustrative Facts.* New York: American and Foreign Anti-Slavery Society, 1853.

Grandy, Moses. *Narrative of the Life of Moses Grandy, Late a Slave in the United States of America.* Boston: O. Johnson Publishing Co., 1844.

Gutman, Herbert G. *The Black Family in Slavery and Freedom 1750-1925.* New York: Vintage Books, 1977.

------. *Slavery and the Numbers Game.* Chicago: University of Illinois Press, 1975.

Guzman, Jessie Parkhurst, ed. *1952 Negro Yearbook.* New York: William H. Wise, 1952.

Harrison, Jesse Burton. "Slavery Debates" *American Quarterly Review* (December 1832).

Henson, Josiah. *The Life of Josiah Henson.* Boston, 1849.

Hinds, Lennox S. "The Police Use of Excessive and Deadly Force: Racial Implications." In *A Community Concern: Police Use of Deadly Force,* ed. Robert N. Brenner and Marjorie Kravitz, 7-11. Washington: U.S. Dept. of Justice, Law Enforcement Assistance Administration, National Institute of Law Enforcement and Criminal Justice, January 1979.

Higginbotham, Jr., A. Leon. *Shades of Freedom: Racial Politics and Presumptions of the American Legal Process.* New York: Oxford University Press, 1996.

Huggins, Nathan Irvin. *Black Odyssey: The Afro-American Ordeal in Slavery.* New York: Pantheon Books, 1977.

Hughes, Louis. *Thirty Years a Slave.* Milwaukee, 1897.

Jackson, Andrew. *Narrative and Writings of Andrew Jackson.* Syracuse, N.Y., 1827.

Jacobs, Harriet Brent. *Incidents in the Life of a Slave Girl.* ed. L. Maria Child. Boston: Act of Congress, 1861.

Janson, Charles William. *Stranger in America 1793-1806.* New York: The Press of Pioneers, Inc., 1935.

Johnson, James Hugh. *Race Relations in Virginia and Miscegenation in the South 1776-1860.* Amherst: University of Massachusetts Press, 1970.

Jones, Rhett S. "Structural Isolation, Race and Cruelty in the New World." *Third World Review* 4, no. 2 (Fall 1978): 34-43.

Jones, Thomas H. *The Experiences of Thomas H. Jones, Who Was a Slave for Forty-Three Years.* Boston: Boyin and Chandler, 37 Cornhill, 1862.

Keckley, Elizabeth. *Behind the Scenes.* New York: Carleton & Co. Publishers, 1868.

Kennedy, Joseph, ed. *Population of the United States in 1860; Compiled from the Original Returns of the Eighth Census, Under the Direction of the Secretary of the Interior.* Washington, D.C., 1864.

Kolchin, Peter. *American Slavery 1619-1877.* New York: Hill and Wang, 1993.

Kulikoff, Allan. "The Origins of Afro-American Society in Tidewater Maryland and Virginia, 1700-1790." *William and Mary Quarterly.* 3rd Series, vol. 35, no. 2 (April 1978): 226-259.

Lane, Lunsford. *The Narrative of Lunsford Lane, Formerly of Raleigh, N.C. Embracing an Account of his Early Life, the Redemption by Purchase of Himself and Family from Slavery* 4th ed. Boston: Printed for the publisher. Hewes and Watson's Print, 1848.

Lerner, Gerda. *Black Women in White America.* New York: Vintage Books, 1972.

Levine, Lawrence E. *Black Culture and Black Consciousness.* New York: Oxford University Press, 1977.

Mallard, R.Q., D. D. *Plantation Life before Emancipation.* Richmond, Virginia: Whittet and Shepperson, 1892.

Maquet, Jacques. *Africanity: The Cultural Unity of Black Africa.* New York: Oxford University Press, 1972.

Marable, Manning. "The Military, Black People and the Racist State: A History of Coercion." *Black Scholar* 12, no. 1 (January/February 1981): 6-17.

Martineau, Harriet. *Society in America,* vol. 2. London: Saunders and Otley, 1837.

McDuffe, Jerome A. *Politics in Wilmington and New Hanover County, North Carolina, 1865-1900: The Genesis of a Race Riot.* 2 vols. Ph. D diss., Kent State University, 1979. <www.1989 wilmingon.com/AlexanderManly Rebecca Felton> (12 Feb. 2006).

Mellon, James, ed. *Bullwhip Days: The Slaves Remember.* New York: Avon Books, 1990.

Morison, Samuel Eliot and Henry Steele Commager. *The Growth of the American Republic.* Rev. and enl. 4th ed. New York: Oxford University Press, 1960.

Morgan, Edmund S. *American Slavery, American Freedom.* New York: W. W. Norton & Co., Inc., 1975.

Morris, Thomas D. *Southern Slavery and the Law 1619-1860.* Chapel Hill: University of North Carolina Press, 1996.

Mullin, Gerald W. *Flight and Rebellion: Slave Resistance in Eighteenth-Century Virginia.* New York: Oxford University Press, 1972.

Myrdal, Gunnar. *An American Dilemma.* New York: Harper & Brothers, 1944.

NAACP, *Thirty Years of Lynching in the United States: 1889-1918.* New York: National Association for the Advancement of Colored People, 1919.

Newman, Francis William. *Character of the Southern States.* Manchester, England: Union and Emancipation Depot, 1863.

Nichols, Charles Harold. *Many Thousand Gone: The Ex-Slaves' Account of Their Bondage and Freedom.* Leiden, Netherlands: E. J. Brill, 1963.

Northup, Solomon. *Twelve Years a Slave: Narrative of Solomon Northup.* Auburn: Derby & Miller, 1853.

Oakes, James. *The Ruling Race: A History of American Slaveholders.* New York: Alfred A. Knopf, Inc., 1982.

Olmstead, Fredrick Law. *Journey and Explorations in the Cotton Kingdom.* vol. 1. London: S. Low, Son & Co., 1861.

Osofsky, Gilbert, ed. *Puttin' On Ole Massa.* New York: Harper & Row Publishers, 1969.

Owens, Leslie Howard. *This Species of Property.* New York: Oxford University Press, Inc., 1976.

Parish, Peter J. *Slavery: History and Historians.* New York: Harper & Row Publishers, 1989.

Pennington, James W. C. *The Fugitive Blacksmith.* London, 1849.

Perry, John C. *Myths & Realities of American Slavery.* Shippensburg, Pa.: Burd Street Press, 2002.

Phillips, Ulrich B. *American Negro Slavery: A Survey of the Supply, Employment and Control of Negro Labor as Determined by the Plantation Regime.* 1918; reprinted Baton Rouge: Louisiana State University Press, 1989.

Pro-Slavery Argument as Maintained by the Most Distinguished Writers of the Southern States. Charleston: Walker, Richards and Co., 1852.

Rawick, George P., ed. *The American Slave: A Composite Autobiography.* 41 vols. Westport, Conn.: Greenwood Publishing Co., 1972.

------. *From Sundown to Sunup: The Making of the Black Community*. Westport, Conn.: Greenwood Publishing Co., 1972.

Redpath, James. *The Roving Editor: Or Talks with Slaves in the Southern States*. New York: A. B. Burdick Publisher, 1859.

Reid, Omar G., Sekou Mims and Larry Higginbottom. *Post Traumatic Slavery Disorder*. Charlotte, N.C.: Conquering Books, LLC, 2004.

Robinson, W. H. *From Log Cabin to the Pulpit*. Eau Claire, Wis., 1913.

Shippee, Lester B., ed. *Bishop Whipple's Southern Diary 1843-44*. Minneapolis: University of Minnesota Press, 1937.

Smith, Danu. "The Upsurge of Police Repression: An Analysis" *Black Scholar* 12, no. 1 (January/February 1981): 35-41.

Smith, James L. *Autobiography of James L. Smith*. Norwich, Conn.: Press of the Bulletin Company, 1881.

Stampp, Kenneth M. *The Peculiar Institution: Slavery in the Ante-Bellum South*. New York: Vintage Books, 1956.

Statistics of the Population of the United States, Embracing the Tables of Race, Nationality, Sex, Selected Ages and Occupations . . . Compiled from the Original Returns of the Ninth Census (June 1, 1870). Wash., D.C.: U.S. Government Printing Office, 1872.

Stroyer, Jacob. *My Life in the South*. Salem: Newcomb & Gauss, 1898.

Takagi, Paul, "Death by 'Police Intervention.'" in *A Community Concern: Police Use of Deadly Force*, ed. Robert N. Brenner and Marjorie Kravitz, 31-38. Washington: U.S. Dept. of Justice, Law Enforcement Assistance Administration, National Institute of Law Enforcement and Criminal Justice, January 1979.

Terrell, Mary Church. "Lynching from a Negro's Point of View" *North American Review* 178 (1904): 853-68.

Thompson, John. *The Life of John Thompson, A Fugitive Slave: Containing His History of Twenty-Five Years in Bondage and His Providential Escape*. Worcester: J. Thompson, 1856.

Thorpe, Francis Newton. *The Federal and State Constitutions*. 7 vols. Wash., D.C.: U.S. Government Printing Office, 1909.

Tolnay, Stewart E. and E. M. Beck. *A Festival of Violence: An Analysis of Southern Lynchings, 1882-1930*. Urbana: University of Illinois Press, 1995.

Truth, Sojourner. *Narrative of Sojourner Truth*. New York: Arno Press and the New York Times, 1968.

Ward, Samuel Ringgold. *Autobiography of a Fugitive Negro: His Anti-Slavery Labours in the United States, Canada & England*. 1855; reprinted New York: Arno Press and the New York Times, 1968.

Waters, Andrew, ed. *On Jordan's Stormy Banks*. Winston-Salem, N.C.: John F. Blair, Publisher, 2000.

Weld, Rev. Theodore D. et al, eds. *Slavery as It Is: Testimony of a Thousand Witnesses*. New York: American Anti-Slavery Society, 1839.

Wells-Barnett, Ida B. *On Lynchings*. New York: Humanity Books, 2002.

White, Deborah Gray. *Ar'n't I a Woman?: Female Slaves in the Plantation South*. New York: W. W. Norton & Co., 1985.

White, Walter. *Rope and Faggot: A Biography of Judge Lynch*. New York: Alfred A. Knopf, Inc., 1926; reprinted Notre Dame, Ind.: University of Notre Dame Press, 2001.

Yetman, Norman Y., ed. *Voices from Slavery: 100 Authentic Slave Narratives*. Toronto: General Publishing Company, Ltd., 2000.

Index

Nigger box, 16-17
North American Review, 132

Obama, Barack, 138
Oliver, Salomon, 84
Overseers, 7-8
Owens, Leslie Howard, 43, 54, 82, 94

Parish, Peter J., 7, 12, 46
Paternalism, 6, 7, 95
Paternalistic,
    compromise, 6
    concern, 15
    ethos, 6
Patrick, Deval, 138
Patrol duty, 43
    fine for non-performance, 43, 45
Patterson, Amy Elizabeth, 86
Peculiar Institution, 4
Pennington, James W. C., 99
Perry, John C., 7-8, 13, 17, 19, 34, 53,
    74, 81, 83
Phillips, Ulrich B., 3, 7, 9, 15, 19, 121
Police,
    repression, 132
    killing of young black men, 133,
    135-136
Polygamy, 111
Post-Reconstruction, 131, 133
Post traumatic slavery disorder, 129
Post, W. L., 23, 46, 84, 132
Powers, Betty, 62, 74
Prayer, 23-25
Praying, 23-25
Pregnant slaves,
    murder of, 29, 68
    torture of, 28-29
Profit, 7, 95
Profits of Farming, 78
Promiscuous bondswoman, myth of,
    109-111
Prostitution, 38
Punishment, 5-7

Race relations, 137
Racism, 9, 44, 130, 131
Raines, Mary, 29
Rape, 38, 46, 51-54, 57-58
    child rape, 63-64
    concealment of, 51-54

as an act of counter-insurgency,
    58
defined, 51
for profit, 81-87
laws against, 51-52, 72
master-on-slave, 57-58, 81-84
of free black women, 61
of house slaves, 62-63
revealed, 57-58
Rawick, George P., 5, 6
Reconstruction, 132, 133
Religion, 21-25
Religious,
    clandestine services, 23
    freedom, 21, 23
    instruction, 4, 22-23, 25-26
    meetings, 23, 26, 45
    worship, 26
Reparations, 137
Resistance,
    slave, 4, 5, 67-68
Rewards, 6, 7, 8, 10, 11, 12, 13, 15
Reynolds, Mary, 121
Robinson, Harriet, 84
Robinson, W.H., 67
Ross, Amanda, 110
Ross, Sarah, 17, 28, 104
Runaway slaves, 39-40, 45

Salt water cure, 17
Simms, Bill, 75
Simms, Dennis, 17
Simpson, Ben, 32, 39, 64, 99
Simpson, Jane, 18, 121
*Slavery: A Problem in American
    Institutional and Intellectual Life*,
    4
Slavery: History and Historians, 7
Slave breeding, 38, 71-78
Slave children,
    sale of, 118-123
Slave codes, 5, 23, 35-39, 43, 46, 61
    barring slave testimony against
    whites, 36-37
    permitting the murder of slaves,
    37-41
Slave Community, 5
Slave clothing, 99-100
Slave family, 87, 93-96
    separation of, 93-96, 115-124

About the Author

A native of Boston, Anthony W. Neal is a graduate of Concord Academy. In addition to an A.B. with honors in history from Brown University, he holds a J.D. from University of Texas School of Law. He is currently a member of the Bar of the Commonwealth of Massachusetts. Mr. Neal has lectured on the topic of civil rights and has been a panelist for Massachusetts Continuing Legal Education and The Real Estate Bar Association for Massachusetts, advising lawyers, employers, and employees on state and federal anti-discrimination laws. He is a community leader, artist, historian, and an attorney of over twenty-two years. *Unburdened by Conscience* is his first book.